# THE DREAMS
# OF
# EBKILFGN

## AN ALLEGORY ABOUT CONSCIOUSNESS

Steven R Tonsager

ISBN: 978-1-946195-93-7

FUZIONPRESS

1250 E 115th Street
Burnsville, MN 55337

*"So the inference was that the energy of the book itself would accomplish its own spread and communication. And, as such, it did, all by itself, with no advertising or promotion."*[1]

[1] Hawkins, David, *The Eye of the I* (Sedona, AZ: Veritas Publishing, 2010), 21.

# *TABLE OF CONTENTS*

INTRODUCTION .......... 1

CHAPTER 1. THE CATALYST .......... 3

CHAPTER 2. INCUBATION .......... 7

CHAPTER 3. ARGENTINA .......... 14

CHAPTER 4. ARIZONA .......... 21

CHAPTER 5. MOZAMBIQUE .......... 33

CHAPTER 6. TIBET .......... 39

CHAPTER 7. SPAIN .......... 53

CHAPTER 8. TIBET REVISITED .......... 69

CHAPTER 9. ECUADOR .......... 81

CHAPTER 10. JAPAN .......... 89

CHAPTER 11. CHINA .......... 94

CHAPTER 12. INDIA .......... 100

CHAPTER 13. KENYA .......... 109

CHAPTER 14. BULGARIA .......... 116

AUTHOR'S NOTES .......... 126

# *INTRODUCTION*

My name is Dolmen Wilcox. I was named so because of my mother's favorite professor of archaeology. One day I married Penelope Fischer. Our life together was not what I expected, that's for certain. My family encouraged me to write this book and share with you, as best I can recall, the travels and experiences that have shaped my life. This book will hopefully be of encouragement to all of you to follow your own path and be open to adventures that you would never have imagined to be possible.

## CHAPTER I

# *THE CATALYST*

I will begin my story with my senior year in university. It was the last lecture for the last class of my last semester. Though the last class was one that held no interest for me, I needed the class so I could officially graduate and have my degree. This evening was to be the final formality of all of the formalities. Fortunately, every lecture for anthropology 101 was optional except the last one. That was not too much to ask—easy, peasy—but if you didn't attend the last class, you didn't collect the credits. It was actually the first and last time I attended the class—the last time I'd attend any other class at the university or any place else, so I thought at the time. I had no intention of ever returning there again. The prior year everything had fallen into place so that my future was neatly laid out in a plan of success. I had succeeded in obtaining a very impressive job with an equally impressive starting pay scale because of my degree in business and accounting. I had also acquired a serious girlfriend and expected that marriage would soon be the next step. Not everything goes according to plan; I didn't know that this particular class would be the moment when so much certainty would vanish.

Dutifully led by the nose, I showed up for the class. It was the first time I saw the professor, who was an old man with large eyebrows and a gentle voice. It took only a few minutes before I fell asleep in class. The next thing I knew, I felt a gentle tap on my shoulder, and it was him. The room was empty. I had slept through the lecture and didn't even wake up as the other students left the hall.

"I don't think we've met," he said. "I am Professor Ebkilfgn. Since you attended the final lecture, you met the requirements and will receive credit for the course."

"I'm so sorry. I didn't mean to fall asleep. I was up late last night and—"

"It's quite all right. Don't worry. Please come up to the front of the class. I would like to show you something."

"Like I said, I'm really sorry."

"Please follow me."

I followed him up to the stage. On the desk sat a notebook with his lecture notes and his briefcase. He opened the briefcase and took out a round wooden box. He opened the box and removed a bowl that was cushioned in tissue paper.

"Take your hands out of your pockets. I want you to hold this bowl."

He placed the bowl in my hands.

"Examine it carefully. Feel its textures. Memorize its shape, form, size, and color. Create a perfect representation of the bowl in your mind. Commit it to your memory so that you can recognize it both by how it looks and how it feels. Have your hands be as certain of its qualities as your sight. Tell me when you know it in this way. Tell me when you know it as surely as if you had fashioned it yourself. Take as much time as you like."

I examined the bowl for a few minutes and felt its contours. I tried to do exactly what the professor said. "Okay, I got it."

"Very well, then," he said.

He went back to the desk and picked up an ordinary looking clear drinking glass filled with water. "Hold the bowl with both hands," he said.

I adjusted my hands to balance the bowl while he poured some of the water into it.

When I shifted the position of my fingers to hold the bowl, my finger scraped a rough spot, breaking the skin. A drop of blood appeared on my index finger.

"Balance the bowl on your other hand," he said. "Dip your injured finger in the water."

I did as he asked. When my finger touched the water, the cut instantly disappeared. The drop of blood in the water swirled and changed shape. I thought that it was dissolving in the water, but in a moment, the drop was transformed into a small red rose.

Before I could say anything, the professor gently lifted the rose out of the water and exchanged the bowl of water in my hand with the rose.

"The rose is for you," he said.

He walked to the edge of the stage and poured the rest of the water from the bowl into a pot that contained a small plant. Then he returned to the desk and put the bowl back in its box before returning it, and his notebook, to his briefcase. He smiled at me in a familiar way, as if he knew me, although I was certain I had never met this man before in my life. He bid me farewell and good luck with my future endeavors.

I thanked him, but before I had a chance to ask him what had just happened, he put on his coat and left with his briefcase. I heard his footsteps as he walked down the hall and the sound of the door to the building opening and closing. I stood there for a moment, not knowing what to think or do about what had just taken place. I held the rose in my hand, unable to explain its origin. I looked at my finger, which bore no sign of any cut or abrasion. When I glanced at the corner of the room where the professor had poured the water in the planter, I saw that the plant was no longer a tiny plant. It had become a huge tree with fruit covering its branches! I closed my eyes again for a moment, wondering if I was still dreaming and class wasn't over yet, but when I opened them, the tree was still there, the rose was in my hand, the classroom was deserted, and my watch said that the lecture had finished nearly an hour ago. I carefully placed the rose in my backpack and returned home.

I lay awake the entire night, unable to go to sleep. I replayed the events over and over again, trying to understand what had taken place. When I got up in the morning, I opened my backpack and took out the rose. The soft, delicate petals left a red smudge on my fingers. It wasn't a strange dream. It really happened!

I decided to return to the lecture hall to try to figure out what had taken place. I looked at the fruit tree and noticed a letter that was nestled in the branches. The front of the envelope bore my name, so I opened the envelope. Inside was a photo of an old man and a young boy. The boy was holding a bowl that looked to be the same as the one I'd held the night before. The old man did not resemble the professor. I turned the photo over, and on the back was written these words:

*The time has come for you to fashion such a bowl. Trust that you have learned enough to accomplish such a task. Professor Ebkilfgn.*

I went home and studied the photo. My daily routines became a secondary priority that day. I went through the motions, the formalities, that were intended to secure my certain future, but I could not stop thinking about what had happened, the photo, and the words of the professor. I went to the offices of the anthropology department to inquire about the whereabouts of Professor Ebkilfgn because now I was filled with questions. The department assistant said there was no professor by that name employed by the university. I protested and demanded to know the name of the professor who taught anthropology 101 this term. She told me that it was an online course and that there were no in class lectures. I told her that didn't make any sense because I had attended the class only a few days ago. She told me that I must have accidentally sat in on the wrong course. She checked my records online and assured me that I had received full credit for the class. When she realized that it was my final class before graduation, she congratulated me on my accomplishments and wished me good luck in my future career.

To say that I was confused would be an understatement. I wrestled with telling anybody else about what had happened before I decided to stay quiet about it and not risk all that I had worked for. I kept the photograph in a secret place.

## CHAPTER 2

# *INCUBATION*

Over the next several years of my life, I orchestrated a successful and unsatisfying career with all the perks as an intelligent businessman. When you think and act in a way that is resonant with this business culture, it really isn't personal. It only seems that way. It's just what happens as a consequence of choosing to identify with the culture's unspoken, impersonal forces. I must say that this life came with what everyone would consider perks.

External success without internal wealth is the same as impoverishment. The two are quickly and easily confused. As a young man, I did not see it this way, but now, as a much older person, I see what happened during that part of my life from a different perspective. Even so, thanks to my external success, my family experienced a life of privilege. My kids had wonderful potential that was cultivated in a world of privilege and with adherence to the guiding principles of most Americans, and Penelope and I experienced many wonderful moments as we watched them grow into adults.

My daughter Lana is three years older than my son Degen, but they formed a wonderful bond that Pen and I cherished. We hoped that long after we were gone, they would remain friends and support each other. We achieved so much of what our parents told us to—a successful marriage and the "good" life: I climbed the ladder of corporate success, and I was an expert at climbing even if my heart wasn't totally in it. Pen was a much-beloved art teacher in her school. Our kids would make anyone proud. They were Exhibit A, living proof, of what good parents we were.

Nevertheless, the photograph taken nearly twenty years ago that I found in the plant after my last class in college did not leave my memory. Over the years, I took it out from its hiding place and recalled the strange events of that last lecture. Did those events really happen?

Although many would say that Pen and I were a template for success and that our children were proof of this fact, I did not feel as successful as others might think. I did not know that the unplanned events of my life would permanently change my definitions of poverty and riches and failure and success. As a young man I often felt that I was lacking something even though our budget allowed us to purchase both what we considered to be fun and what we considered essential.

I couldn't forget the photo the professor gave me despite the passing of so many years. The picture only reminded me that I would never feel content until I did what he told me: I needed to fashion my own bowl.

It was time to try to do something to eliminate this nagging request that never would completely leave me. I finally decided that it was time to take action. I needed to respond in some way to the photograph. I told Pen that I was going to take a pottery class. I knew that would surprise her—this was not what she would expect from her ladder-climbing husband.

She responded, "Really? Why? Well, I hope you enjoy it. Maybe you can make some new wine glasses. You could use a hobby, something to do when you're not working."

I was neither discouraged nor encouraged by what she said, and I didn't change my mind. I signed up for a community pottery class for beginners. On the first day of class, we were asked to introduce ourselves and share our reasons for our interest in making pottery. I did not tell the teacher or the others about my real reasons for being there. Even if I wanted to do so, it would have been difficult—at that point, I really couldn't have explained it to myself! Why did the teacher need to know that I was embarking on a mission impossible? It would have helped if I knew more about my assignment than the words Professor Ebkilfgn spoke to me several years ago:

*"The time has come for you to fashion such a bowl. Trust that you have learned enough to accomplish such a task."*

How could I possibly bring it up to these strangers as we went around the room, each of us taking a turn at telling the others about our decisions to take a pottery class? I didn't think that it served any useful purpose to say that I was there because of a photo. What would the teacher say? "I don't quite understand. Please explain." Instead, I made up some predictable answer to fit in with the others, a harmless, safe answer.

I began to learn to shape factory-produced clay that was made to help beginners shape something that would not easily fall apart. I found that I actually liked working with clay and that I was not bad at pottery making, for a beginner. Outwardly, I was on a path to learn about how to shape the clay, but in truth, I was there to reshape myself. That was my secret. I admitted to enjoying the class, enjoying immersing my hands in the slimy mixture of the clay with the possibility of creating something new.

I sat at the wheel working with the clay, and it took me back to that day in the lecture hall. I was certain that I was far afield from accomplishing the task that the professor gave me. I didn't understand yet what he really wanted me to do. I had not yet realized that there was little, if any, connection between the bowl I held on that day in the lecture hall and the conglomeration that was spinning on the table and being shaped by my hands, but I enjoyed the class. For reasons that I couldn't explain, it seemed to connect me to the magical day in the lecture hall.

There were other tangible benefits to pottery, which Pen pointed out to me. She told me that making pots seemed to relax me. That was true. It gave me something else to focus on besides work, which seemed to help me balance some of the daily frustrations of work. I became sufficiently interested in the activity that my pottery-making activities were worthy of the description "hobby." I took another significant step in my hobby when I used some of our fun money to purchase my own pottery-making equipment. I built a shed in the backyard to be solely used for pottery. I even purchased a small kiln. I think that Pen was pleased with these developments. She told me that I was more relaxed and positive, and it was all from throwing pots, I guess.

Sitting at the wheel gave me the solitude to think about my new hobby and its connections to the rest of my life. I became something of a serious student of my new hobby, although I had yet to know in my soul what any of it had to do with what had happened so many years ago in that classroom. I couldn't forget the professor's words, no matter how many pots I made.

The brief encounter with the professor left me with many unanswered questions. Although I didn't have any answers, I believed that the professor's bowl beckoned for exploration of its meaning. I decided to put my considerable intellectual gifts to the challenge of understanding the chemistry of clay and the making of pots. I left no stone unturned. I studied the history and mechanics of pottery until my technical skills and my understanding of the chemistry of clays eventually rivaled my ability to do the accounting for a complex business.

This led me to make even better pots. Though many of these pieces were of professional quality, to my great disappointment, not a single one of them evoked the same feeling within me as when I held the professor's bowl. I was doing what he told me to do in trying to fashion my own bowl, but I knew that I had not succeeded in fulfilling his intent. I did not know what was missing or what else to do to improve my pottery skills. As a person who was used to being successful at everything I tried, it was frustrating to know that I had not done what I set out to do.

With the rest of my life, it was business as usual—it was just "busyness." The security and benefits of my successful career were not very satisfying. I was busy, but not engaged in my work. I felt like the owner of a lead balloon, not a golden parachute. Sometimes I shared my frustrations with Pen during our evening ritual of drinking wine and reviewing the events of the day.

When Pen asked me what I thought the problem was, I couldn't really tell her. I didn't know the problem, myself. There was so much about our lives that was perfect, and the kids were launched. Our daughter Lana became a nurse, and she wanted to work overseas to help the poor—she was always an idealist of sorts. She was exceptionally happy about meeting David Nellman at a church she was attending. David was an engineer who was interested in construction projects for the disadvantaged overseas. It was, by all appearances, a perfect match for our daughter. They told us that they had applied to work in Africa through an organization that was sponsored by their church. They expected that their application would be accepted. Our thoughts about them being so far away were mixed. Time would tell.

Our son Degen was nearly finished with graduate school. He was a plant geneticist who would soon be entering the workforce with a small bioengineering firm in Washington. We were proud of both of them.

Pen asked me, "Don't you like your job anymore? Is that it?"

I said, "Maybe what I chose to do as a college student was right for me then. After all, look at what it has done for us and our children…I just don't know what else I would do now. Besides, I don't want to risk what we have worked so hard to attain."

Pen replied, "It seems like you're more interested in pottery than being at the office, but you seem frustrated by the pottery too, even though you're practically a professional. Is that what you want to do? Be a potter?"

"No, Pen, I don't want to be a potter. I just know something is missing in my life."

"Like what? Is it me? Are you unhappy with me?"

"No, it's nothing like that. I want to show you something."

I went into my office and retrieved the photo I'd received from the professor. I handed it to Pen.

"What's this?"

"I received this picture on the last night of class when I went to my anthropology lecture senior year. Read what's on the back."

She turned the photo over and said, "I don't understand. What has this got to do with anything that we are talking about?"

I explained everything that happened to me on the night of the lecture, now almost thirty years ago. I was afraid to tell her, wondering what she might think, but I also was relieved because it felt like I had been carrying a secret all this time and it was time for the secret to be shared.

Pen said, "Why didn't you tell me about this before? Why did you keep it a secret?"

"I didn't know what you would think. You could have thought I was crazy. I don't know. I really didn't know what to say or how to handle it. I'm sorry."

"So this is what's behind the pottery making?"

"Yes."

"Have you fashioned the bowl you set out to make?"

"No."

"Maybe it's not possible."

"I have wondered that, too."

"Maybe we need a vacation, just some time to be together, to get away from work and the pottery shed. Let's go on a trip."

"I think that's a great idea. I'm sorry for keeping this photo from you. I'm sorry."

"It's all right, darling. I think if I had been in your shoes, I might have done the same."

"Do you believe me?"

"I don't know what to believe. It's so far beyond anything that has ever happened to me that I don't see how it's possible. Maybe you were dreaming; I don't know. It doesn't matter. I'm glad you told me about it. I love you and I believe in you. You're a good man. I am happy for our life together…I think it's time for a vacation."

We talked about many destinations and eventually chose Argentina. We planned a wine tour in the Mendoza region, an area near the Andes

Mountains that was known for its fine Malbec wines. The anticipation of the trip lifted our spirits.

I did not suspect that this diversionary trip held more in store for me than some wine tasting or that this vacation would move me so far away from my safe and predictable life. The trip to Argentina was like going to Cape Canaveral, putting on astronaut gear, and being hurled into outer space. I didn't know that you could travel to another planet without leaving Earth.

## CHAPTER 3

# *ARGENTINA*

Before we left, we did what most intelligent planners would do: We researched Mendoza, Argentina and worked with a travel agent to develop an itinerary that would fill two weeks with wine, adventure, and a trip to the Andes Mountains. Being our first trip without our children, this was new territory for us. Pen and I were infused with the anticipation and excitement of our first vacation as empty nesters. Everything unfolded as we had scripted it from our computer and with our travel agent. We didn't want to be part of a tour group, so it would be just the two of us. We hired our own personal guide to take us wherever we wanted to go.

After a long flight, we were in Buenos Aires. A bus took us to the terminal at Mendoza. We met our driver, who took us to the first hotel of our trip. It was all as we had planned. It was a beautiful place, spectacularly beautiful. Seeing it with our own eyes enhanced the many photos of the region we had viewed on the Internet. The next day, we enjoyed the first of many enjoyable days travelling to visit the many wineries throughout Mendoza province. We followed our itinerary, just as we planned, with the help of our driver, who reliably brought us to every stop. We were having a marvelous time. Pen was right, a vacation was exactly what we needed. Our trip was nearly half over when one day, on our way to the next town on our itinerary, a sign caught my eye for another winery that we had not planned to see. I didn't recall seeing it listed on any web page, but I was intrigued to add one more place to visit.

Our guide said, "Not many people know of this one, but I am happy to bring you there."

Pen was not opposed to a change in the schedule. After all, it had already been an amazing trip. Our driver took us to this little winery that was not on the radar for most travelers. It turned out to be a momentous choice.

It was a beautiful setting, and soon we were sitting at a thick wooden table on an outside patio, tasting another wine and gazing at the Andes.

I started to feel strange. I felt a bit light-headed. I thought that maybe I'd had one too many glasses so early in the day, so I got up to move around and get some fresh air. I accidentally bumped into a man who appeared to be a local customer.

"Excuse me," I said. "I'm sorry."

He smiled at me, extended his hand, and said, "Don't worry about it. Are you all right?"

I shook his hand and immediately felt an intensification of this peculiar light-headed sensation that I had attributed to the wine. I couldn't tell you why, but my mind immediately transported me to that anthropology classroom. It was the sensation I felt when I held the professor's bowl! How could that be? That didn't make any sense.

I returned to the table, not quite myself, and Pen asked me if I was all right. I looked back to point out the man to her, but he was gone. We stayed for a few hours, but the man did not return. I decided to not tell Pen about what had happened. Why would I? I wasn't sure what had just happened!

I slept very little that night, despite all of the wine. I got up to use the toilet and then washed my hands. As I looked at my hands, I saw the image of a rose on my palm, calling to mind the connection to the professor from so many years ago. This was too strange for words. I went back to bed. Maybe I was drunk or dreaming.

In the morning when I awoke, I went outside to inspect my hand more closely. I did not see the imprint of the rose any longer, so I realized that maybe I did imagine it. As I stared at my hand and thought about the encounter with the man the day before, a young woman carrying a basket greeted me. From her basket, she drew out a single red rose.

"Share it with your wife. It will be good luck for the next day of your vacation," she said.

I thanked her and went upstairs, where I shared the rose and a romantic time with Pen. We dressed and went downstairs for breakfast. I told her how much I enjoyed this vacation and especially this place. I wasn't ready to leave the town we were in. I wanted to try to figure out what was happening to me. I needed more time there to think about the strange sensation I'd felt when I bumped into the stranger and shook his hand. I'd seen an image of a rose on my palm the night before, but the rose on my hand was no longer there. All of this beckoned to me to stay another day. I asked Pen if we could go back to the winery we visited the day before.

"But we have our itinerary," she said. "There are plenty more places to see."

"Yes, I know, but there is something quite magical here and I would love to stay another day and try to figure it out."

"Very well, then," Pen said. "It is an adventure, after all, isn't it?"

We explained to our tour guide that we decided to stay an extra day. He didn't understand why, but he was accommodating since he was being paid well. We were his only customers, so it would just be a day of not much driving for him.

We returned to the winery in the midafternoon. It was peaceful. Music played as other wine tasters came and went. Soon the winery was quite full, a hum in the air. I was looking around, trying to spot the man I'd bumped into yesterday, but I didn't see him. Pen and I were engaged in conversation when an older couple interrupted us and asked if they could share the table with us.

"My name is Pablo Ramos, and this is my wife, Calde."

We got acquainted and shared more wine. Pablo said they lived a couple of miles from the winery, out in the country. They'd retired from the University of Santiago, Chile and moved to this quiet place several years ago.

"It sounds lovely and peaceful," I said.

Calde replied, "If you would like to see it, then why don't you come to our home tomorrow for a visit? If you have time."

Before I could answer, I was surprised to hear Pen say "Yes, we would love to come. What's one more day of changing the schedule?"

I was pleased that she accepted the invitation. How I loved my Pen!

Our driver took us to their home the next day. It was a lovely drive and an enchanting place.

We were welcomed by a young woman I recognized from the hotel. It turned out that she was their granddaughter, Elle. She worked in town; she'd given me the rose the day before!

The four of us stayed up late into the evening, drinking more wine and sharing stories.

Pablo Ramos was a seventy-one-year-old retired professor of ancient history who taught at the University of Santiago, Chile. In his study, there was a picture of a man who resembled Professor Ebkilfgn. Pablo informed me that this man had been his favorite teacher. Somehow, seeing the picture assured me that I was in the right place. I contemplated the unlikelihood, the mathematical improbability of being in their home and looking at this picture that night, so far removed from our original travel plans. I thought about the irony surrounding the possibility that I might be exactly where I was supposed to be.

Pablo sensed my surprise and amusement.

Then he said, "Yes, of course it is peculiar, my friend. It is as if we have been friends for a very long time, although we just met. You think you know where you are going, and then you take a detour, an unplanned departure from the schedule, and now this."

He laughed. "And now you think that you are exactly where you were supposed to arrive in Argentina, after all of your careful planning. Yes, it is an engaging thought!"

Pablo walked with a slight limp due to an injury to his hip when he was thrown from his horse. He told me that as a young man he was often reckless, an out-of-control gaucho. The injury could have been more serious.

"Now I am thankful for this hip trouble. It was a gift because it led me to leave the life of a gaucho behind me and enter the university. Imagine that, all from an old injury."

Pablo said his early life was filled with foolish adventures. "My desires led me around by the nose. I was the rider, but the horse was in charge. I knew I needed to get off that horse, or one day I might not have the chance to do so."

I enjoyed listening to Pablo. He spoke earnestly about his mistakes but didn't make excuses for them. He saw each adventure as another step in the process of bringing him closer to what he was really after, even if he would not get there on the back of a horse.

The more I listened to him, the more I felt he was not only a wonderful storyteller, but also a storehouse of knowledge and facts befitting a university professor. Pablo possessed a different commodity—I call it wisdom. This wisdom was not about how much you knew, but what kind of a person you had become. That evening, I felt like I was being introduced to someone I would like to emulate. Pablo was a teacher, healer, and lover of humanity. I'd even call him a visionary and prophet. As such, he motivated his students with the fiery inspiration to move forward on their own. Now I felt inspired by him just by being around him.

We were so thoroughly welcomed into Pablo's home and the chemistry between the four of us was so powerful that they invited us to spend the night. We talked late into the evening, under the stars.

I was surprised when the next morning, Pablo took me out to his pottery shed. It was a wonderful surprise to discover that we shared this interest. He explained his hobby to me as play time that nourished his soul. He collected many kinds of pottery, and he enjoyed collecting clays from his many travels. He brought them to his studio and experimented with them to develop new textures and appearances.

I inspected several pieces as he explained where the clay used in each piece was from and the techniques he used to work with it. My eyes were drawn to a series of bowls and pots on one particular shelf.

"May I?" I asked.

Pablo replied, "Yes, of course. Please feel free to pick them up as you wish."

I picked up a pot that reminded me of pottery made in the southwestern United States. When I held it in my hands, I felt power surge through me. While the pot did not physically resemble the professor's bowl, the feeling was familiar.

"One of my favorites," he said.

"Where does the clay for these pieces come from?"

"It is from Arizona, from an area near a river that was home to a tribe of Indians for generations."

"How did you find out about this clay? How did you acquire it?"

He laughed and said, "What would you expect from a professor of history? Actually, a student of mine from many years ago knew of my interest in Native American history. She told me that her mother was Indian. I told her about my interest in pottery, and she promised she would give me a pot."

He continued. "One day after class she gave me the pot you are holding. I liked the feeling of this pot very much and asked her if it would be possible for her to send me some clay. A few months later, I received a letter and a package of clay from her—a great gift. The letter explained that the clay came from a spot known only to her mother's relatives. She said they dug some of the clay just for me, and I felt very honored to receive it."

I really liked the feeling of the pot. It felt special to me and possessed a quality that I could not describe. I wondered if I needed to use a different source of clay in my own pottery. Perhaps that was why this pot was the only one that felt this way to me even though I had handled several of Pablo's pieces. This was the one that was different.

Pablo said, "All of the clays have some story to tell. Isn't it interesting that you chose this one? Maybe you needed to hear that story."

Our time was coming to a close and we needed to bid each other farewell. We were getting ready to leave when Pablo said that I should take the pot with us. It was a gift from him and a symbol of our new friendship. I protested only mildly because I really did want the pot.

The depth of our new friendship with Pablo and Calde was like none we had previously known in our lives, despite having so many connections back home. It felt so good to share the experience with my wife. Pen also felt how special this place was. It was not long before we were back home, and we had many stories to share.

I put the pot in my study and then shared with Pen both how special the pot felt to me and its origins. I was certain that it would not be long before we headed to Arizona.

# CHAPTER 4

# *ARIZONA*

Going to a small Indian reservation on vacation is not exactly the same as using the established services of a travel agency to visit wine country in Argentina.

I wasn't sure what I was looking for, but I explained to Pen that I wanted to dig some of that Arizona clay for myself and work with it in my studio. I told her that I felt a strong connection to the pot that Pablo's student gave him. Pablo gave me the pot and told me to discover the story of the clay, and I didn't know that clay had a story. All I could say to Pen was that I wanted some of the clay for myself. She was up for the challenge. We would prepare ourselves for another adventure.

The reservation land was dominated by a casino and its satellite services. This was the modern-day revenue generator. It seemed at odds with the spirit of the land and with the people who had lived here less than a century ago. We rented a jeep and spent the day driving the dusty roads and getting a feel for the place. We inquired about pottery making and stopped in a few small tourist shops. No one seemed to be able to help us find clay.

We stopped at a small broken-down Protestant church and learned that a few people showed up there once a week to learn pottery the old-fashioned way. We thought of returning later in the week to see if someone could help us find our own supply of clay.

It was getting late, so we headed back to the room we'd reserved at the casino, since it was the only place for outsiders to rent rooms on the reservation. We were encouraged to avoid leaving the casino after dark. The manager was friendly and assured us that everything we might need was available in the room or could be ordered from the casino.

This was not a quaint setting. It was loud and felt chaotic, although the chaos was managed and renamed as excitement. “Come to the casino and you, too, can be a winner.” Here, you could get wine out of the box.

There was no wine tasting there. The manager told us the best meal in the county was available at the casino, but the smoky atmosphere quickly rewarded Pen with a headache, so she excused herself and went up to our room.

I could not sleep, so I went back downstairs and walked through the noisy casino, which was filled with gaming tables and slot machines. *Why not*, I thought to myself. I played a couple hands of blackjack and lost. There was nothing enjoyable about giving my money to a card dealer who probably gave most of it to the owners. That made it easy to leave the table and walk away.

I took my free drink to the bar, where I downed one more drink, and one more as I pondered how to find the clay. Everything exceeds its natural appeal when it is seen through the eyes of someone who has had one too many.

A woman was watching me while I sat at the bar. She came over and sat down next to me. I was easily attracted to her, so we made an arrangement to continue the conversation in a more private place. I think the alcohol took over my negotiation skills and decision making.

April was her name. She had jet black hair, ornate jewelry, and a beautiful body only slightly concealed under a nearly transparent dress. I followed her to a room in the hotel, way past a boundary that I had respected for many years, but before the boundary was fully breached, I was saved by a higher power.

She undressed with her back to me. I saw a rose tattoo at the base of her spine. A second tattoo sat in the middle of her back, a drop of blood surrounded by concentric circles. The third tattoo, on her upper back, spread across her shoulders. It was the image of a tree with fruit on its branches.

I was immediately brought back to my senses. Those tattoos carried a message that even the spirit of alcohol could not hide from me. Each tattoo reminded me of what happened to me the day I dipped my bleeding finger into Professor Ebkilfgn's bowl. This could not be a coincidence.

I said, "I'm sorry, April. I'm very sorry. I don't think this is a good idea. I've changed my mind. Please get dressed and keep the money. I'm really sorry."

"What's wrong?" she asked. "I like you. I want to give you what you want. I want to give you what you paid for."

I knew that no matter what she said, I wasn't going to change my mind. I was thinking about her tattoos. I could not ignore the message. It felt like my life depended on it. I knew I was supposed to meet her but not screw her. Now all I wanted to do was find out more about who she was.

I said, "You're beautiful, and your tattoos are very interesting to me. I know this sounds strange, but they are actually giving me a message. I would really just like to talk. Could we go downstairs and just talk for a while, please?"

She studied me and then said, "I'm not looking for a boyfriend or a sugar daddy. I know you're married. Look, you already paid me, so let's do what you planned on doing when we came up here. I know it wasn't just talking."

I replied, "You're right. Like I said, I changed my mind."

"Why?"

"Because your tattoos are a sign that I was supposed to come to Arizona to find the clay."

"What?"

I did my best to explain to April what I meant, and she agreed to have a conversation. I decided to tell her why Pen and I were at the casino while she got dressed. I explained to her that I came here to dig for clay, not fool around, and told her about being in Argentina and the pot

Pablo gave me. I wasn't sure what she thought about what I was telling her. We went back to the bar.

April told me about her life being raised by her grandmother. Her grandmother's name was Beki, and she was one of the few remaining members of her tribe who knew how to make pottery according to the ancient ways. The chemistry between us changed as we talked about her life outside the casino.

My interest in Beki grew with each story she shared with me. I could tell April enjoyed telling me about her childhood and her relationship with her grandmother. When there was a pause, I gently interrupted her and told her I would love to meet her grandmother.

"Yes, I think she would like to meet you too," April said. She gave me a pottery shard from her purse with the image of a coyote painted on it.

"My real name is Lehithee, but you can call me April. Give the shard to my grandmother when you see her. She will know that I have sent you to see her and you will be safe. She will understand and help you to find the clay."

"Thank you very much, April. I am honored to meet you, and I'm sorry about what happened before."

"There is nothing to be sorry about. I was not offended, only surprised. I hope that you find what you came looking for so far away from home."

"Yes, thank you again."

"Now we are friends instead of anonymous sex partners. Give my best to my grandmother."

"I will."

I'd lost track of time when I was with April. I did not know that Pen came downstairs and spotted me talking with April. She decided not to let me know she saw me and watched from a distance as I accepted the shard and put it in my pocket. Pen was puzzled and bothered by what she saw and left without me knowing she was ever there. She returned to our room and waited for me, many thoughts racing through her mind. The meeting with April created a huge conflict that took Pen and me a long time to resolve, but if there was anyone to blame for the problem, it was definitely me.

When I got upstairs, Pen was not asleep.

"Where have you been? What were you doing? You were gone a long time."

I selectively told Pen what happened, leaving out all the incriminating details. I explained that April shared her grandmother's information with me and told her about the shard to show Beki so that she would know her granddaughter trusted me. I told Pen this would allow us to find the clay.

She nodded but said little. I could tell that she was not satisfied by my answer.

Then she said, "Are you telling me everything? I feel like there's more to the story. Is there more?"

I lied and told her that this was what we came to find out about. I was afraid to tell her the truth. I think she already knew that there was more to the story. I was not sure if she was disappointed in me for holding back or just plain angry.

The next morning, we set off to meet April's grandmother. It was not hard to find her place. She was sitting in a chair on a small porch when we turned into her driveway. We got out of the jeep and walked up to the edge of the porch steps.

"Good morning," I said. "Are you Beki?"

"Yes, I am Beki. Why are you here?"

I handed her the pottery shard April gave me and said, "Lehithee gave this to me and said you would help us."

Beki said, "Where did she give this to you?"

"At the casino."

"Oh, at the casino. She would not have given this to you if you had been with her for the same reasons most men have when they meet my granddaughter." Beki smiled at me. I think she probably knew that my meeting April did not begin with as much innocence as she was inferring with her words. She knew Pen was monitoring all of the cues, not just Beki's words. Beki was wise and gracious.

I thought I was completely safe, and then Beki said, "You saw the story on her back, didn't you? It is your story. That is why you have come for the clay."

"How did you know about the clay? Did she call you? Did you know we were coming?"

"No, she did not call me. It is all over your face. I expected someone here this morning, and here you are." She laughed.

I was caught completely off guard by Beki's words. I did not know what to think or say. I wondered what Pen was thinking. Did Beki see right through me? I was surprised that I did not need to explain myself or rationalize my actions to Beki. Apparently she already knew the story due to some inner wisdom. It was gracious of her to not require me to spell out every detail. I felt her encouragement, her acceptance of my frailties, and most of all her kindness, even if I deserved none of it.

The tone of the conversation changed, becoming less intense as she told us about her love for the earth and her connection to the clay. I delighted in her stories about walking the desert as a young girl with her mother and learning how to feel for the clay with her toes. She told us about what it was like when April lived with her as a child, how she took April to the places where she'd learned to feel for the clay through her feet. Beki told us that April was always interested in her pots. Sometimes she came with her to dig for clay and helped build the fires.

Then Beki said, "And now it is time for you to find the clay."

She described the location of the clay and gave us directions. Beki also warned us that the desert could be an unforgiving place if you didn't know how to handle its harsh conditions. She told us to be careful.

We thanked her and left her place to head back to the casino. We would leave in the morning to gather the clay. Her directions sounded simple enough even though there were no road numbers or signs. I remember how excited I was about getting the clay. I also remember how good it felt to meet Beki; I believed that I was aligned with a deeper purpose. We were so close to the place Pablo's student had gotten that clay. I felt like the events of the last two days were a confirmation that I was on the right track.

The next morning, we headed off to get the clay. It was already getting hot outside, but inside the jeep it was very chilly. We drove down a dusty, unmarked road, and it got hotter outside and even colder inside the jeep. At first we rode mostly in silence, but not the kind that feels peaceful while you are just enjoying the ride. The atmosphere was unpleasant, awkward, and uncomfortable. The air needed to be cleared for both of us to breathe easily. I knew the silence would only last for so long, so I tried to think through and construct my best defenses and my best arguments because I was certain that I would need them to defend myself. In my heart, I knew I was guilty. The more I thought about it, though, I realized that this was not correct. I was not guilty. I was clueless. I needed Pen's forgiveness, but I wanted her compassion. I wanted her to tell me that if she had been in my shoes, she would have acted no differently. I didn't want a "not guilty" verdict. I wanted her love and understanding. I thought that would move us forward. I hoped that I might offer the same for her, although these were just words and I didn't really know what that act might entail.

I knew that it was not my virtue that kept something from happening between me and April. It was an act of divine grace. I knew it. Pen knew it. I didn't want to be punished. I desperately wanted her love, her patience, her steadfastness. I was lost in my thoughts as we drove down unmarked roads in search of the clay.

After a time, words erupted out of the volcano of silence between us. Perhaps it would have happened anyway without any awkward conversation between us, but we got lost. We got very lost. To make matters worse, we ran out of gas. *Damn!* What else could go wrong? How could I possibly get myself into even more trouble?

When the argument occurred, it was a full-blown eruption. Hurtful words were spewed and tears flowed as we stood outside the useless jeep hurling accusations and rationalizations alike.

"You could see her tits through that dress. What were you doing with her in the first place, asking about clay? Oh, bullshit, you were. I know what you were going to do. When were you going to tell me the whole story about how you met April? *You just saw her and asked her about clay.* You are such a liar. How can I trust you?"

We were on the border of civilized and uncivilized conversation when the gods smiled upon us. Our yelling and screaming was interrupted by the sound of an approaching car. A young Native American man asked what we were doing there.

"You are trespassing on my land," he said. "This is sacred land."

I apologized and asked if he could give us some gas, offering to pay him extra for his troubles.

He reluctantly agreed. As I told him why we were out there, he acted disinterested, perhaps even angry that we were on his land, but then I said that Beki had sent us here for the clay. His countenance changed. All of a sudden, everything was okay—no actually, everything was much more than okay. It was as if he had been dispatched by Beki to help us.

After he filled the tank with gas, he said, "If Beki sent you, then I don't want your money."

He pointed to the place she had apparently been telling us to go. If this was not a sign from the Holy Ones, then I doubt I will ever recognize one. Even Pen was calmed by his words, sensing that something was going on and looking beyond the thought of me cheating on her. Even though I made a serious mistake in my initial reason for meeting April, that meeting was leading us to a gift that I didn't deserve but needed to accept with gratitude.

I uttered the word Beki had spoken to me in her native tongue when she'd pointed to the spot on the horizon where the clay would be found.

The young man said, "This is a sign. I will take you there myself."

I noticed a necklace around his neck. The pendant had a wooden figure of an antelope.

"What is your name?" I asked.

"I am Hekeke."

He pointed to a mountain that was several miles from our present location. "That is where Beki means for you to get the clay."

I held out my hand and shook Hekeke's hand. I felt the sensation that I was beginning to understand, an energetic confirmation from the Great Unseen of a purposeful meeting. I could tell by the way Hekeke reacted that he also received a divine confirmation of his decision to bring us to the clay.

We followed his car along another unmarked road, and another, and another. When we arrived at the place he'd designated, Hekeke told us how much clay to take, how deep to dig, and how much time we had to collect it, as well as the safest way to leave this sacred land. He said he would watch us from a place known only to antelope until it was clear that we had completed what we had set out to do.

He spoke some words to us in a language that I did not understand. When I asked him to tell us what he said, he simply replied that it was a blessing. I would have liked to ask him so many more questions, but I could tell that this was not possible. He would not take my money.

"Beki would not allow it," he said.

"Why? I don't understand."

Hekeke said, "Money will cheapen the clay and what I have done to help you. The clay cannot be bought by man. It is a gift from the Great Spirit."

Before I had any chance to argue, he was back in his old, dusty vehicle and speeding away.

Eventually, Pen and I conversed more about April. We found some peace, but at that time it was more like a cease-fire agreement. My impulsiveness was to blame for the new tension in our relationship. It was irrelevant that my actions led us to the clay. I was torn by the experience. I wondered if I would have ever met April's grandmother, if I would have ever found the clay, if I had not met her. Even so, it created a new challenge for me to work out with Pen. I know the clay was not a reward, but one more example of the grace of our Creator, the Great Spirit, or whatever name we might offer to acknowledge that we are not alone.

Pen was doing her own thinking about this trip, too, about how different it was from our time in Argentina and how quickly the excitement of going to the desert to continue the adventure had been extinguished by what had happened at the casino. She knew me well, which meant that there was a whole lot more going on than sex. I apologized and Pen forgave me. More importantly, she eventually recognized that there was something else that was going on in my life. She did not withhold herself from me, but every time a beautiful girl was in our vicinity, I felt her disappointment in me—or at least I thought I did. This could also have been my own doing, my own issues, which she did not take on as her own.

Pen did not deny the magical encounters and synchronicities that were taking place. She didn't call me foolish, stupid, or superstitious. Maybe this was the very best thing she could give me, because it did not discourage my quest for a deeper understanding of my own life. This only made me love her more. I hoped that more time would make for more gentle moments between us. I hoped that I could give her the same grace that she gave me, and I felt immensely thankful about being Pen's husband.

We returned home to our routines and the expectations that came with them. I thought that some time without so much drama was just what we needed. Pen was back to teaching her art classes and I was back to crunching numbers for our clients, although there was some clay in the shed that I could hardly wait to fashion into pots.

I thought a lot about Beki and April. I also thought fondly of Hekeke. Whenever I thought of April, I did not only think of how beautiful she was. I thought about April digging clay with her grandmother, the laughter between them, the clay in their fingers, the connection between her feet and the earth. I wondered what kinds of stories were shared. I thought about Beki and her hesitation to use words for anything except kindness. I thought about Hekeke telling us that no one could buy the clay, that it was foolish and even insulting to the Great Spirit to think to do so. Despite all of the troubles of the trip, mostly brought by my own decisions, I was very glad that we went. I was very glad.

I loved Pen. I did not wish to be with April, but I was grateful for our meeting. I thought fondly of her, appreciating what she shared with me so that I could meet Beki. I felt compelled to continue the process of giving thanks for the unexpected gift of encountering people who meant more to me than I could have imagined.

Pen also taught me about love as she surrendered her grievances. Time afforded me the gift of forgiving myself and becoming a better person. The antidote to arrogance is humility, and the experience helped me to be more understanding about the drama that is called daily life. After this trip, I was less inclined to volunteer my opinions about the lives of others. I remembered the speck and the log story from Sunday school when I was a kid.

Thinking about my life in this way was a valuable lesson. I had April, Beki, and Hekeke to thank for being such good teachers. I had Pen to thank for making it real and transformative, for making sure that I stayed after school to do my homework.

When I was not working at the office, I was immersed in the clay that we had gathered in Arizona, doing the best I could to apply these lessons. I knew there was a connection between the potter and what he made with his hands. I knew that I was just getting started. It was likely that I would make more foolish decisions, but I felt that the Great Spirit would fashion it all for good. At this time, that was enough to know that I was blessed.

# CHAPTER 5

# *MOZAMBIQUE*

Penelope and I were blessed with two amazing children. Isn't that what most parents think? Our son seemed to be the more practical child, while his older sister was much more of an idealist—or so I thought. How does any parent know? How does a parent separate their wishes for a satisfying life from the inherent nature of a child?

Both of our children were encouraged to follow their dreams and work hard to achieve them. While we surely influenced their goals, there were always some surprise decisions that reminded us that they had their own ideas. One such surprise decision was that Lana and David became involved with a healthcare organization that did relief work in a village near the Zambezi River in Mozambique that was known for its history of devastating floods and healthcare challenges, including AIDs.

We Skyped to stay in contact. We were proud of their tenacity, courage, and compassion, and we knew that she went there with David to make the world a better place. It was an effort sponsored by their church. Knowing our daughter, we knew it wasn't about conversion; it was about providing help to those in need. They accepted a three-year commitment to be there.

While they were there, they had their first child. They named her Ida. Not long after that, they told us that Lana was pregnant again with a second child. Our daughter convinced her mother and me to make the trip to Mozambique to be present around the time of the due date. We made the long trip.

The trip to Africa to see them was a good thing for us. I don't remember a lot of the details about the flights after we landed or the logistics of getting to such a distant place, but I do remember how tired I was when we arrived. What I remember most about this trip, besides the birth of our second grandchild, was a young man named Bi (pronounced bee).

Bi was sixteen years old and a member of the local tribe. He was the son of a fisherman, and his mother was a medicine woman and thrower of pots. He assisted our daughter and her husband in their work, bringing medical supplies and bartering for other necessary things. I am not sure if I would use the word beautiful or handsome to describe his features, but he was slender and swift and powerful, like a young lion. He could have been a warrior or a ballet dancer. Flexible, agile, and graceful, he ran like a gazelle and walked like a princess. He seemed under the spell of a different purpose than the other men in his village. Lana told me that he was a dual spirit, but I did not know what she meant by that.

When our daughter and her husband abandoned the practice of distributing the church's educational materials and accepted the traditional beliefs of the people, everything changed. David and Lana decided to be simply themselves—two loving people guided by compassion to love others. It was a lot simpler than what the church was asking them to do. "We just want to love them," Lana said. Our daughter was known by the title Beautiful Rose because she seemed to bring a gift to all she met.

A few days after we arrived I was overcome by a bout of dysentery. Lana told Bi to ask his mother to prepare some herbs for me. Bi went to fetch the water from a special well, and the herbs were steeped in the special water and mixed in a bowl that she'd made. Bi delivered them to me.

I could not help but think that Bi was sent to help me remember who I was and that my life was actually fulfilling a purpose, even if I remained mostly clueless about what that purpose was despite some unusual events. When I grasped his hand, once again I experienced a sensation that I was learning to trust as a divine touch. I felt the familiar affirmation that we were of the same origin. As his mother prepared the remedy, he showed me the pots his mother used to cook the herbs and the water from the well that he drew for her to prepare them.

The fact that Lana had asked for the tribe's help in treatment was another confirmation of what Pen and I had talked about so many times as we wondered about how David, Lana, and the baby were getting along so far away from home. Their compassion and humility about their work and the respect they shared for the medicine and culture of the local people moved us. We were proud of what they were doing through their work, but we were learning, too, and letting go of some of our cultural assumptions about what the word "civilized" really meant.

I felt that was a confirmation of how we had raised Lana, and I encouraged her to think about herself and others. Pen and I thanked God for the gift of knowing all of the villagers and being chosen by Lana to bring her into the world. Our visit to Africa somehow brought us back into sync again. I do not know, nor would I try to explain, the mechanism for this reconnection. I was simply grateful that Pen encouraged me to keep making my pots. She professed her belief in me and our involvement in something too big to understand from any one person or experience. We had a night that we had not had for many years.

We experienced a healing and an unexpected fondness for Mozambique that we would have not known if we had not taken the risk, the journey. I was healed of much more than dysentery by the collective energy of the community that had become David and Lana's community.

I didn't know how our time there would fit into a bigger picture. All that I knew was that what I thought I knew was being gently changed. Nothing was being forced upon me through a sales pitch to join a different religion; I just liked how it felt to be with these people.

What could be wrong with that? If that was wrong because it wasn't Christian, then that was too bad. Being there taught me the difference between being a spiritual person and belonging to a religious group. I concluded that being a member of any religion was no guarantee of having good qualities in your heart. My experiences in Africa helped me realize that a religion with a very different background than my own could also be overflowing with the gifts of the Spirit. When I thought about my church back home, I knew that many of its members would not agree with me. They would say that the people in Mozambique were lost without Christianity and that it was their job to "bring them to Jesus." I thought that my new friends had more to teach me than I could ever teach them.

Let me tell you about another incredible experience in my African classroom. One day I watched Bi as he went to a quiet stretch of the river. I heard him say something in another language, although I couldn't understand it. He looked up into the sky and laughed, and then he closed his eyes and swiftly thrust his hands under the water. He lifted a large fish out of the water. He held it up in the air in front of him and spoke more words that I did not understand.

He put the fish in a basket he'd brought. Bi saw me, smiled, and said, "It is a gift from MIRRI for all of us to be nourished."

I wondered how he'd caught that fish. His eyes reflected the sky and the waters. He was connected to his world in a way that I did not understand since I had no comparable experience from my personal history. I was fascinated, intrigued, and ignorant about any explanation that could help me understand how Bi could pull a fish out of the water as he had done! I would not call what I had witnessed "fishing." Not only was I reminded of how little I knew about my own skills, but also of how inadequate I felt about my lack of understanding about how things really work.

Our scientific understanding of nature is not the truth, only a different belief system. The system in which Bi operated was no less valid than what was praised as advanced in the so-called civilized world. This led me to consider how our ways of understanding the world encouraged society to see the water, the soil, and the sky as inanimate, lifeless material, but Bi and the people of his village knew otherwise. Yes, I thought it was true that we have lost our connection to the water, to the sky, to the soil, and to ourselves.

The next day I asked his mother about what I saw and how it was possible to pull a fish from the water with only his hands.

She replied, "MIRRI is the creator of all things, even you. There are no differences between any of us if we understand this. Some, like my boy, not only believe what the elders have taught them, they know in their hearts that they, too, are MIRRI. They feel and see it. Behind every appearance, there is only MIRRI. My son is the sun and the water. He is the plant, the rock, the bird, the lion, and the fish. The fish knows this too, and that is why it swam into his hands."

She could see me struggling to understand what she had just said, so she said, "It is not strange to me. It is only strange to you, sir. We see things you do not see. You can't see it because you don't know what it looks like, yet it is always there before you."

I wanted to learn more from her. I asked her if I could watch her make pots, but she said that it would not be right to do so. I asked her if I could accompany her when she picked her herbs, but she again politely refused. She did, after some pleading, furnish me with a satisfying answer as to why that gently and clearly ended my request.

I'd never told her anything about my own pottery activities back home, but she said, "You have already learned how to make beautiful pots in your own country. You will not find what you are seeking from watching me do these things. I know that MIRRI is helping you. Think about this when you are back home making your pots: MIRRI will guide you. That is how you will find what is missing. Do not worry, because Bi and I will bless you. We are servants of MIRRI. When you put your hands in the water one day, the fish will find you."

I was stunned by what she said to me. How did she even know that I made pots? More than ever, I was glad to be here, even though I had become so ill. If I had not, would I have learned these things about Bi and his mother? I felt that these "primitive people" had more to teach us than the civilized world could ever teach them. This was a place of higher learning; the classrooms were simply disguised by grass and mud. I was pretty certain that these people possessed more wisdom than I would ever accumulate. They knew more about what really mattered than I could possibly ever know.

The day came for the birth of our second grandchild. The medicine woman served as Lana's midwife, and I watched him enter the world and be bathed in the waters of the Zambesi River. Lana and David named him Doren. I watched Bi bring the water to wash the baby. I could not have imagined more holy or more precious water than what Bi gathered, blessed, and shared. I thought how fortunate it was for Doren to be born here.

Once again, I felt that this trip meant more than what I could have possibly imagined. Each of our trips was part of one larger journey of self-discovery. I wondered where the overall journey would take me, and I felt that despite so much uncertainty and so many unanswered questions, I was exactly where I was supposed to be. This was a thought that acquired more prominence in my way of viewing the unfolding of my life as time went on. I felt that same peace and joy about my daughter's life and choices.

What difference does it make if we call this author of so grand a plan God or MIRRI? I thought about how important Professor Ebkilfgn's words from so long ago had become for me. I heard them expressed in a new way through Bi and his mother. I felt an urgency in my soul to know MIRRI in my daily activities, to feel no sense of separation between myself and the world as it was for Bi, to be one with my surroundings, or to be simply one, without subject or predicate. I wanted to feel MIRRI and the sacredness of the land and its inhabitants, to know MIRRI as the clay and the power of the clay that allows it to cohere.

I was lost in my thoughts. I wanted to understand and experience this oneness with everything more deeply, more personally, like Bi and his mother. I wanted to pull my own fish from the water for the benefit of all. The clay was not an inert material. It was alive, like the water that talked to the herbs and encouraged my body to say goodbye to the diarrhea.

The clays that I dug in Arizona were just other parts of my body, but through the limitations of my perception, they had been reduced to inert materials to make pots. These clays, too, were MIRRI. Yes, there was much to think about.

# CHAPTER 6.

## *TIBET*

The trip to Mozambique also profoundly affected Pen. She returned home with a sense of relief that our daughter and son-in-law were well and safe. She was proud of them, as I was, but Pen also said that she felt some sense of personal emptiness, like she was not as powerfully engaged in her life as Lana and David were in theirs. "I return home to teach art. Is that it?"

We talked about her feeling of not being in tune with her purpose. Yes, the art classes benefitted others and yes, she still enjoyed it, but something was missing. Being in a different culture sharpened her vision of her own culture, and she diagnosed herself with a severe case of cultural myopia. The expansion of her context and consciousness was an unexpected gift from our visit to Africa. Pen was back to her familiar routines, but they had become too familiar—maybe even stifling. I encouraged her to keep thinking outside the box about what she knew and was comfortable with in order to find her own personal truth.

"The answers will come soon. MIRRI will make sure of it," I joked.

"MIRRI? Really?"

"Just kidding." As I listened to myself say these words, I knew that I really wasn't kidding.

I knew that Pen would pull her own fish from the water. At that time, I had no idea that the fish that Penelope would soon pull would have Tibetan fins. I did not know how Asian cuisine went with Argentinian wine or elephant dung tea, but we would soon find out.

As we settled into life at home, I spent less time making pots and more time thinking about what Bi had done and what his mother had said. Penelope decided to follow her own signs to the river; one day she told me that she was enrolling in a class to help her become a more soulful painter. "Someone who paints with a purpose," she said.

"What do you mean?" I asked.

Pen said, "I want to feel more connected to my own art and my paintings, not just teaching art or the mechanics of painting. There is so much more to painting than how to hold a brush, how to mix colors, or what stroke to use."

"Where is this coming from?" I asked.

"I attended a seminar given by a calligrapher who explained that the drawing of the characters was a spiritual process, that it was soul work.

"I can't tell you exactly what the difference was between him and me, but when I listened to him and watched him paint, I knew that he was connected to what he said. I know that something is missing in my painting. I want to paint as he does!"

"So what happened next?" I asked.

Pen continued. "A woman in the audience asked the question that I was going to ask. 'How do we learn to do what you do?' He said it was not another technique, but that we would have to work on our hearts. He said that true painting comes from being connected to the heart. The audience was very attentive. Then I spoke up and said, 'But there must be someplace we can start.'

"'Yes, that's true,' he said. 'My son teaches classes not just for painters, but for people like yourselves who want to have their hearts awakened and feel more connected to who they are and what they do.'

"Someone else asked, 'What do you call this teaching?'

"He said, 'It is a kind of energy work that marries your body and mind to one another and to all things. Your culture lacks the word to describe it. I will leave the information with you.'"

As Pen shared her experience of the seminar, I could feel her enthusiasm. Of course I would encourage her. The class was less than an hour's drive away, which was a lot closer than Arizona.

The class turned out to be just what she'd hoped for and needed. My wife was an enthusiastic student and practiced diligently all that she was learning, forming new bonds with like-minded people in the class. She told me about her new discoveries, how energy moved differently in her body, and especially her hands, when she painted. She learned to meditate. She said that she felt healthier and more positive about her art and her job.

I was happy for her. And then came the surprise.

"I have something I want to talk to you about," Pen said. "I want to go to Tibet to continue my studies. My teacher told me that he has reached the limit of what he can teach me. He is encouraging me to go further, to fulfill my potential. With his recommendation, they can arrange for me to learn from his master. I would very much like to be an apprentice there."

"Can I come with you?" I asked.

"No, it's not allowed. I did ask, but they told me that this would interfere with my training."

"For how long?"

"Three months. I really want to go, but I will not go without your support."

We discussed it more. I eventually agreed to a compromise: After the three months, I would come to visit and learn about what she had accomplished firsthand, perhaps even travel and escort her back home. I silently worried that her new adventure might create distance between us.

"It makes me nervous to think of you being so far away with no possible way of contacting you."

"I understand, but please don't worry. I will be fine."

There was still more discussion. A few days later, she let me know that my wish to come visit her after the three months would be allowed.

The next several days were filled with preparations for her trip and more discussions about the importance of Pen following her path and me following my own. I was doing my best to be as enthusiastic about her plans as she had been for mine.

A couple of days before she left, I said, “MIRRI has many names, don’t you know? What do they call him in Tibet? When you are finished, I expect you will tell me.”

She smiled and said, “Yes, Dolmen, maybe I will come home with another name besides MIRRI.”

I felt uncertain about how the apprenticeship with her teacher’s master might affect our relationship. What would it be like when we reunited? Would she still be satisfied with our marriage? Would she say that there was something missing between us? Would she need to go somewhere away from me to find it? I kept wondering if there was some way to have at least a small amount of contact with each other.

“Can we Skype or exchange letters?”

“No, it is a remote location and not allowed. No contact is allowed, per the master’s instructions. My teacher will contact you through an intermediary, as he promised, four weeks before you will come. Then you will have time to make all of the arrangements to come to Tibet.”

It was more than hard to say goodbye. I did not know what the future would hold, and I was too small to laugh and look up at the sky and say, “It is all well, MIRRI.” I said my goodbyes at the airport and returned home to an empty house. This felt very different than freely chosen downtime for myself. I was uninvolved in a great time of excitement and adventure for Pen.

The next day, I drove an hour to the town and the building the classes were held in, and then I went to a nearby coffee shop to wait until the classes were open. While looking at the flier for the art classes outside the coffee shop, I met an interesting man. I thought he was probably there very early for the next class, just to make certain that he wasn’t late. He followed me into the coffee shop.

"Are you taking the class?" he asked. "It doesn't start until seven. Do you mind if I join you?"

He was friendly, but I was preoccupied with my own reason for coming—to investigate what might influence Pen so powerfully to put our life on hold and go to Tibet. The man didn't seem to notice my lukewarm response. He extended his hand. I wouldn't have looked up at him or even given it a second thought—I was absorbed in my own thoughts—except that when he shook my hand, I felt a powerful but now familiar surge of energy. I had come to know that the surge of energy at the joining of our hands was significant, an important sign that something important was on the way, even though I didn't know what, why, how, who, or when. It was that feeling that I was learning to recognize that both excited and settled me internally. Yes, I was in exactly the place where I was supposed to be. I needed to trust what was taking place, including all of the uncertainties that I was feeling about Pen's trip.

I excused myself to the bathroom to compose myself and formulate some questions for him, but when I returned he was gone. I left the coffee shop and went into the building where the classes were taught. The next class was already underway. I waited outside in the hallway, not wanting to attract any attention to myself. Eventually, the class finished and I saw a few students leaving, but I did not see the man in the coffee shop. Where was he?

I went inside the classroom and stayed in the back of the room. I eavesdropped on the conversation between the man I presumed was Pen's teacher and a female student. I listened and watched while a part of my mind began to weave a fantasy of classroom romance between him and the student. I heard her say how much she looked forward to the next class. She said something about how she never felt energy flow through her body like this, and my ego made sure that I would turn this into something it was not—a very personal, intimate conversation between a teacher and an attractive female student. All it did was make me think about Pen.

First I wondered. Then I worried. I had no basis for feeling this way; my own fears fueled this insecurity. Soon, the student excused herself and I approached the teacher.

"Good evening, Mr. Wilcox. May I call you Dolmen? It is a pleasure to meet you."

"How do you know my name?"

"You are exactly as Pen described you."

His eyes met mine and I felt as if I was going through the checkpoint of an airport.

He already knew quite a bit about me. Apparently Pen had told him about me. My survival instincts kicked in, but I maintained my composure and remained calm on the outside. I wondered if he could see through my insecurity or sense that I worried about Pen's relationship with him.

I said, "So you are Penelope's teacher? It is a pleasure to meet you. Penelope would not be doing this apprenticeship if not for your class. I guess I have you to thank for it, or to blame for it. I admit this was more than I thought she was signing up for."

My mind raced; I was starting to lose my composure. I could find out the real truth, but the main conversation was going on within me; the teacher was just there like a piece of furniture. My thoughts were moving at a lightning pace, energized by the baseless allegations my mind conjured up so easily. I wondered what Pen would think if she saw me here, or if she would think I was questioning her loyalty to our marriage.

I felt embarrassed. I asked him something about the class in general and then tuned out, not listening to what he said as my mind completed another lap of high-speed foolishness. *Do you feel better now?* How so? *Having seen him?* I don't know what you mean! *He was handsome, fit. I saw how the other woman swooned.* Was it the same with my wife?

I finished another mental lap while he answered my superficial questions, and then I got out of the race car and managed to put my feet on the still ground.

I struggled to say, "I just wanted to meet Penelope's teacher, to understand what's going on."

Inside I knew that was a lie.

He was kind to not call me out on my unspoken assumptions. No doubt he had been in this situation before as he talked with the partners of his students. Pen and I had a solid relationship, I thought. I had nothing to worry about.

Then he said, "She is awakening to her purpose, just as you are to yours."

He may have been right, but I didn't like hearing it—especially from him. Nor did I like the idea that he seemed to know so much about her and me. Pen had never said that I was a subject of conversation. I felt exposed. I wondered how many times she had stayed after class. It was hard not to get back on the racetrack and run more mental laps on the fuel of negative thoughts and hostile fantasies.

"Do you have the travel information for me?"

He replied, "That won't be available until four weeks from the completion of her training. Didn't Penelope tell you?"

Before I had time to do anything else, I was back in my race car. I heard myself say, "Does that mean you don't have it, or are you saying that even if you have it, you won't give it to me until then?"

I was surprised at how my words were coming out. I was out of control, and my car was travelling at too high a speed. If I didn't slow down quickly and get a hold of myself, I would hit the wall. There would be a big crash, a serious accident. I was embarrassed about both what I said and my tone. I took my foot off the accelerator and quickly apologized.

"I'm sorry for saying that. I guess I'm just a little anxious about what is happening. I don't feel I have any control over what is going on with Penelope. She has never been away like this without me."

Finally, I had managed to say something that approached honesty and vulnerability. I had found a way to slow my car down to a safer speed.

He wrote something down on a slip of paper and handed it to me. "Please don't worry. I understand. Come after class back on this date and I will have the information for you."

There was no change in his countenance, and he remained gentle and pleasant. I left and went home.

I resolved to put all doubts behind me and trust what was happening for Pen as she had done for me. I knew there was plenty for me to do, to think about, and to discover within myself. I knew little about the interconnectedness of all things compared to Bi, and he was only a teenager. The brief moment in the coffee shop was a good reminder of that point. The next day I would make another pot. I would choose to be encouraged by the handshake in the coffee shop. I would try harder to spend less time mentally visiting the racetrack.

Two months passed by more quickly than I expected, and exactly four weeks before the completion of Penelope's training, I returned to the building in which the classes were held. All of the signs and notices on the building for the classes were gone. I went inside and walked down the hall to the room I'd spoken with the teacher in, but it was empty.

I went to the main entrance and asked the security guard about the classes.

He said, "You must be Mr. Wilcox."

"Yes, I am."

"There is a letter for you, and I am supposed to give it to you."

"How is it that you know my name?"

"I was told that somebody with your name would be here today to retrieve this letter."

He wasn't able to answer any other questions.

I took the letter and walked over to the same coffee shop I had visited exactly two months ago. I opened the letter, which said that Pen's training was not complete. The letter stated that I should come back to the building in three more months for my travel instructions. The news of this postponement stunned me. I felt like I was being invited back onto the racetrack again. I wondered what was happening in Tibet. Was Pen all right? There was nothing I could do; I had no other contact information. I had no way to find her or her teacher.

I told myself that panic, frustration, and anger would not bring Pen back any sooner. I was oblivious to what was going on around me as I tried to figure out if there was any constructive action possible. In the midst of this confusion, I felt a tap on my shoulder.

A voice said, "I haven't seen you in a couple of months."

I looked up, but could not place the man.

"Don't you remember? I saw you come over here to wait for the art class three months ago."

Then I recognized him and remembered the energy of the handshake. What an odd coincidence to see him there again at that moment! I asked him if he knew anything about the class or the teacher, but he didn't know anything. I thought it more than a little strange to have seen him a second time. Not only had he remembered me, but without invitation, he found me at this table. I became suspicious.

I wondered if he was in on some kind of scheme with the teacher.

Then he said, "Something seems to be bothering you. Would you like to talk about it?"

He was a stranger, but who else did I have to talk to? I decided to explain the little that I knew about the Tibet situation and share my surprise and disappointment regarding the news of the unexpected delay in seeing my wife.

"Maybe her work is just taking longer," he said. "I wouldn't worry about it."

I didn't feel any better after he said that.

"Why don't you take a vacation?" he offered. "Take your mind off things. Sounds like you could use one."

"Look, I'm sorry," I said. "I need to go."

I just needed to get out of there and think. I didn't want to answer any more of his questions. As if he was reading my mind, he immediately replied, "Exactly. You don't know where to go next."

Before I stood up, he stood up and pulled a business card from his pocket, saying, "I think I know the destination for the best vacation you could ever have. I've traveled a lot, and I keep extra cards for this travel agency in my pocket so that I have one if I want to share it. You never know when you'll wish you had it, although I rarely share it with anyone…But I will share it with you. Give them a call; I highly recommend them. Don't hesitate. This will be just what you need."

Without looking at the card, I accepted it and put it in my coat pocket, thanking the man.

"You are welcome, and good luck. Please call them."

With that, I returned home.

Feeling less solid than I had in a very long time, I reviewed the activities of the day. I thought about what it had been like to be without Pen for so long. I tried really hard to feel sorry for myself without much effect. I lay in bed that night for a long time, but I couldn't sleep. Perhaps the man was right; I did need a vacation. I got out of bed and retrieved the card from my coat pocket. It read EBK Travel Agency. The line below the title promised, "Providing one-of-a-kind vacations for the chosen." There was a phone number, but no address. EBK

Travel Agency! Really? Am I going crazy? What is going on? Who was that man at the coffee shop?

For the next several days, I made the hour-long drive to the coffee shop, but there was no sign of him. There were no posters or business cards for this travel agency. Finally, I decided to call the number. A computerized system asked for my name, address, and billing information so that arrangements could be made for the trip. I entered my information. The system then asked for my credit card information. I hung up before entering that because I was too worried about the risk of sharing my financial information with a recorded voice. To do so would be a violation of every business principle upon which I had built my financial reputation and security. It was my way of being in the world that kept boundaries in place that ensured my comfort and calmed my fears about the future, but this practice didn't seem to be working so well any longer.

This was too crazy. Why would I give a company I didn't know my financial information without knowing what the trip would cost? Only an idiot would do such a thing! Was I getting back on that mental racetrack again by not only saying but doing impulsive things? I was managing so much panic and anxiety below the surface! Why would I go on a trip to an unknown destination? Why would I give them my home address, my credit card information? I didn't even know where I would go or if I would ever return! Confused, but intrigued and possibly on the verge of spinning out of control and crashing, I decided to sleep on it. I would try to figure out my next step after some much-needed sleep.

I experienced a night of fitful sleep and woke up remembering a dream.

*I was lying on my back in the sand near an ocean, but then I got up and walked along the beach. In the distance, there is a herd of cattle. Leaving the herd, one large bull walks down the hillside toward me. He is not just moving in any general direction; he is certainly moving toward me. I move and the bull adjusts its direction to zero in on me. I think he is getting ready to charge me. I start to run and the bull adjusts its pace once more, though he is not fast enough to overtake me. Before I collapse from exhaustion, I stop and face him. The bull stops. I walk toward him and get on his back. We walk to the edge of the water, close enough that the bull can bend over and take a drink, and then the bull moves back to join the rest of the herd. He lowers his head and I dismount. I crawl about on all fours. I eat the grass and smell the clover as if I am one of them. In the distance I see a group of cowboys riding our way. They have come to lasso me. I look down and see that my hands and feet are now hooves. There is a woman under the tree closest to my herd. She is collecting flowers. I move slowly toward her. When I get close enough, she pats my head. The cowboys seem satisfied that I am no longer a stray. She will take care of me.*

I decided that day, for reasons I could not explain, that I must make this trip. I couldn't attribute this decision directly to the dream, but I was hoping that the dream was some kind of message whose meaning would eventually become clear on the trip.

This time I called the number of the travel agency and provided all of the requested information, including my name and my credit card information. This was a complete violation of all the advice I had ever given to my financial clients, but I did it anyway. The system said I would receive the vacation information in one week, which would give me time to free up my work schedule. I could make all of the personal arrangements necessary for wherever this trip would take me.

I decided I should tell somebody what I was going to do, so I told my son about the travel plans. I thought Degen was the best person to inform about my plans in case I never returned, since he was always clear-headed and practical as well as very intelligent. He asked me reasonable questions, and for each reasonable question, Degen received an unreasonable but predictable answer. ("That is no answer," he would reply to my responses to each of his questions.) Our conversation went something like the following:

"Where are you going?"

"I don't know."

"What will you be doing on your vacation?"

"I don't know."

"How did you find out about this?"

"A man in a coffee shop gave me a card."

"And who is this guy? Do you even know his name? You don't even know his name."

"You're right, Degen. I don't know his name."

Then my son said, "This makes absolutely no sense."

Of course, he was right. It didn't make any sense.

"The fact that Mom's staying an extra three months in Tibet doesn't mean you should get crazy. Please reconsider. It sounds suspicious and potentially dangerous."

"I am going to go, Degen. I need to go."

"I wish I could change your mind."

"I know."

My son called the next day. "Dad, I checked the Internet and called several travel agencies. Nobody has ever heard of this travel agency! I hope you didn't give them any personal information like your credit card number."

"Yes, I did."

Degen got angry with me. "I can't believe my own father, who taught me how to plan so well for every contingency, is doing this. I love you, Dad, but please don't go. I'm really worried about you. What you are planning to do is way outside your comfort zone."

"I need to go, son," I said. "I will contact you when I reach my destination and let you know when I will be coming home. I love you, and I ask for your support. I need to do this even if you don't understand what the hell I am doing. I know that I am not able to answer any of your questions. I can't explain to you why, but I need to do this. Please be there for me…And you're probably right; I don't know what the hell I'm doing."

The interesting thing about the conversation with my son was that it took place some distance away from my mental race track. My thoughts were calm during this conversation. Within my soul, I decided that I really wanted to go. I needed to go. I allowed myself to believe that something unexpected was waiting for me, not any of the negative possibilities Degen thoroughly outlined in our conversation.

With Penelope so far away, daily life was difficult. Lana was on the other side of the planet and Degen was left wondering if his dad just abandoned all of the principles that made our family so successful. The dream was playing games with me, though, and it lightened my mood. I did feel like a bit of a stray, like a cow that had wandered far away from the security of the herd.

The itinerary arrived as promised. I learned that I was taking a flight to Madrid, and from there I would fly to another location within Spain and take a train. When I arrived at the destination, I would be picked up in a taxi and be taken to the headquarters of the agency.

I called Degen and told him I was headed to eastern Spain. I tried to reassure him by adding that I would furnish him with as much information as I could when I got there.

"Good luck, Dad. I hope you find what you're looking for. I will meet you at the airport when you return. Be safe. Seeing you do this is new territory for me, too. It makes me nervous, but I believe in you and—"

"It's okay. You don't have to say anymore. Thanks Degen. I love you too."

# CHAPTER 7

## *SPAIN*

One long flight and then a second shorter one followed. I boarded a train and took a wonderful train ride through country that was unfamiliar to me, looking out at mountain ranges, vast plains, cattle ranches, and even vineyards. Cowboys on their horses and large herds of cattle stood scattered across the countryside. I just sat back and watched the scenery, wondering what was coming next. I got off the train and approached a young man holding a sign that read EBK Travel Agency. My driver's name was Pedro. He took my suitcase and put it into his car, and we got in and drove the last few miles to our destination. The agency headquarters looked like a small motel situated on a ranch.

The owner of the travel agency greeted me at the entrance.

"I am Señora Valasquez. Welcome. We have been expecting you for a very long time. We are pleased that you are finally here."

That didn't make sense to me. They'd been waiting for me for a long time? I made the arrangements only a few days ago. Maybe that was the way she welcomed all the visitors in order to make them feel special, I thought.

Señora Valasquez's appearance was striking. She was beautiful. I guessed that she was probably at least sixty, but she was radiant and youthful with dark skin, black hair, a strong nose, a broad chin, and large, dark eyes.

I followed her into the main building.

She said, "You have already met my son, Pedro, who brought you here. Now I want you to meet the others who work for the agency."

There were only three others. One of the staff reminded me of Elle, Pablo and Calde's granddaughter in Argentina. She showed me to my room on the ranch.

The room was bright and clean, but small. There was a bouquet of flowers on a small table and a single bed. The room overlooked the dry, dusty countryside. I saw cattle in the distance.

"There is time before dinner for you to freshen up from your trip." She brought me a glass of water. "Welcome, Mr. Wilcox."

"Thank you, but please call me Dolmen. What is your name?"

"My name is Juanita. Señora Valasquez invites you to join the others at 7:00 p.m. for dinner."

"I am looking forward to it."

After freshening up, I went downstairs and into the parlor to join ten other guests. One of the staff brought wine for us. Soon Señora Valasquez invited us to come into the dining room, where she joined us to complete the table of twelve. Her staff served a wonderful dinner. The other guests were so friendly with each other that I wondered if I was the only newcomer. I said little, observing, listening, and sizing everyone up.

Midway through dinner, the señora interrupted the conversation and said, "Please return here to this table for breakfast tomorrow before departure."

"Where are we going?"

She replied, "That is not something to think about right now. It can wait until morning."

A familiar-looking man who spoke with an Eastern European accent agreed. I couldn't place him, but I was sure I had met him somewhere—the voice was too familiar. I couldn't imagine how I might have ever met him, though. When dinner was over, the other guests bid farewell to the señora and each other. The man with the memorable voice was the last to leave.

He looked at me and then spoke to the señora, saying, "I am glad he is finally here to join us." Then he left.

Just the señora and I were left in the parlor.

She said, "I'm not quite ready to retire to bed yet. I think I will have another glass of wine. Would you like to join me?"

"Yes, I would like that very much."

We went out to the patio.

"I can see that you have many questions. I will answer some of them, but for other questions, you must find your own answers."

"Thank you, Señora," I said.

She replied, "From now on, call me Medir. I am Medir Valasquez. I will tell you some things that may help to put your mind at ease. When does worry ever get us anywhere we want to go?"

Her voice was soothing and reassuring.

She continued. "No one seems to know exactly when it happened but we were given this place centuries ago by Señor Ebkilfgn, a friend of my ancestors. "

I almost dropped my wine glass. "What did you just say?" I could not believe what I just heard.

She smiled as if she knew something and expected this response from me. She shared what she knew with me:

"My husband and I loved this place. I grew up here, in this very home, as a child. It has been in our family for generations, longer than anyone can remember."

She laughed and said, "I think it is as old as time."

She continued with her story. "I've always loved everything about being here. When my husband died, I decided to stay here to continue welcoming travelers. This is what I do. I am so fortunate to know my purpose for being born here! And now, Dolmen, you are the newest traveler."

"How do people know about this place?" I asked.

Medir explained that an awareness of this place begins in a world that is invisible to most people. "Sometimes the first clue to its location begins in a dream. The dream births an intention. When the time is right, an invitation is sent. We know that everyone who comes here has been invited. My father said that we should never worry about who comes for vacation. They think they are choosing to come, but God is actually sending them here. My husband said that even though Señor Ebkilfgn died long ago, God kept him assigned to the task to give the orders to come here. I don't understand it, but he still sends them to us. It has been this way for hundreds of years, maybe more.

"So welcome, Dolmen. We are pleased to have you here for your vacation. Know that there is nothing to worry about. I wish you a deep sleep. See you in the morning."

I returned to my room and replayed the conversation in my head. What would Degen or Lana think of this? How could this be possible? Could the professor and Señor Ebkilfgn be related or even one and the same person? He must have died long ago...Medir said that he'd died, but that he still sent travelers to her. That was what she said!

He sent them there so they could complete the dream. What could this possibly mean? "This is how my father explained it to me," she'd said. "And it is how I explain it to you, to everyone who comes here." I kept thinking about her words. What did it mean that I had arrived there in the same way as every other traveler? I could hear Medir's voice inside my head saying, *I am so glad that Señor Ebkilfgn sent you here, Dolmen. It is part of your journey.* I fell asleep with this in my mind.

The next morning when I came down for breakfast, there was only one place setting at the table, not twelve.

One of the staff served me breakfast. I was almost finished eating when Medir came out of the kitchen.

"I hope you feel refreshed and are ready for your trip."

She took my hands. I felt her warmth and her affection, as if she was holding my heart. It felt as if I was a calf that was being brought back to the herd. Once again I felt that unmistakable feeling of recognition and confirmation in her touch that I was where I needed to be. How could this be possible?

"Where are the others?" I asked.

She replied that I was the only guest making the trip today.

"I don't understand. What about the other guests? Aren't they going too?"

Medir explained, "They only came last night to bless your vacation, your journey, and your work. They are dear old friends and travelers who have all been blessed by Señor Ebkilfgn. Pedro and Juanita will be taking you on your trip."

"Where are we going?"

"To the *balnearios*, the springs," she said. "To the place where all vacationers must go."

Behind Medir I noticed a clay pot that seemed to have some connection with my work in the potting shed back home.

"I see that you are admiring the pot behind me," she said, following my gaze. "It is interesting that it catches the eye of all who sit at this table. Señor Ebkilfgn told my husband that every guest will notice it." She laughed. "Don't ask me to explain why. I don't know."

I asked, "Where did you get that pot?"

Medir said, "I think the answer to this question is already known by your heart, even if you can't vocalize it. There will be a time when you can put it into words and say it out loud."

I wanted to tease her. "Riddles so early in the morning, and I barely finished breakfast? Usually on vacation, the brain gets to take a break." Then I suggested, "The pot was a gift from Señor Ebkilfgn."

Medir nodded not just with her head, but her whole being. When she gazed at me, I felt like we were in a perfect rhythm. Her good intentions caused my heart to vibrate in full resonance with her.

"Yes, Dolmen, of course; you know—and that answer only required your heart, not your brain. Now, you have a long journey ahead of you, and we like to keep all of our guests on time."

"And full," I said.

She laughed. "You need to finish your breakfast."

She sat with me while I finished my breakfast. I asked her if she was a potter.

"No," she said. "Not everyone needs to make pots, though everyone needs to learn what they are made of."

I asked about the clay in the pot that caught my attention.

She said that clay could be found everywhere, that it was only a matter of knowing how to look for it. It was hard not to like Medir. I thought that Pen would like her, too. Medir mentioned that Juanita enjoyed pottery.

"I think you might find her work to be interesting," she informed me. "What is a trip for you without finding someone who knows how to make pots? I look forward to your return."

Pedro, Juanita, and I set off on horses and traveled for many, many miles. The horses needed little direction. We rode in a peaceful silence, and I took in the beauty along the way. I was glad to be making this trip. It was nearly sunset when we stopped.

Pedro said, "This is where we will stay for the night. We will arrive at our destination tomorrow around noon."

Pedro pointed in the distance. "If you sleep with your body facing in that direction, the stars may speak to you."

"Thank you. I hope we all sleep well. Thank you for bringing me here."

That night I dreamed of a river, though I didn't think that it was the Zambezi:

*I wade out into the river, but this time I do not try to pick up any fish. I can feel that a fish is swimming toward me. It swims past me after lingering near me for a few moments.*

A new day began. It was a half-day's journey to reach the *balnearios.* Again we rode in silence as I enjoyed a kind of contemplation that was filled with the sounds of birds and the bellowing of cattle.

Pedro said, "We are almost there."

In the distance I saw a large stone structure. Pedro pointed in the direction of the stones.

He said, "The springs are just beyond the stones." We tied up our horses and I followed Pedro and Juanita through an archway formed by three enormous boulders.

I thought I knew something about the relationship between Medir's son and Juanita. It turned out that I was glad I'd said nothing. When we embarked on this trip, I wondered if they were romantically in love; as we rode together in silence, I soon realized that it was a different kind of love that carried them along the trail. It was obvious that there was a deep bond between them, but it was not an exclusive one. I now felt bonded with them as we traveled together. It was our intention to go to the springs, and that held us together in a single moment. As Medir hinted yesterday, the answers were always available and accessible through my intuition. I imagined that our three hearts were beating uniformly and our horses were stepping together in perfect cadence, as if an invisible leader was entraining each step.

My thoughts were interrupted when Juanita said, "I remember the first time I came here. I had only finished my degree at university in computer science when I received an invitation to come here. One afternoon, while I was sitting by myself in a park, a man approached me and encouraged me to accept the invitation that was printed on a business card. I did not know where the invitation came from, but I was brave enough to call the number as you did, Dolmen, and follow the instructions. I was not sure what would happen next. The card was probably like the one that you received, yes?"

I showed her my card.

Juanita replied, "Yes, the very same." She smiled and continued with her story. "Three years later, and I am still here. I have been waiting for another sign, and now you are here, Dolmen. This is the sign that I was waiting for. I can feel it."

I think Medir must have known this too. I did not know exactly what she meant.

The three of us walked through the huge stone opening and followed a narrow path through the dense vegetation that took us to the *balnearios*. I smelled sulfur. I could hear the sound of water and the singing of the birds, and I felt what I can only describe as a powerful, soothing energy in this place. Like the voice of a male bass singer, but so many octaves lower than any man could sing. I don't know any other words to describe this feeling except a kind of reassuring hum. The smell of sulfur grew even stronger.

When we approached the spring, Pedro said, "We will leave our clothes over here."

Without reservation or embarrassment, both of them took off their clothes. I was caught off guard and a bit nervous, so I told them I would join them in a moment. I watched them walk the remaining thirty yards to the spring. Their bodies were beautiful and young, much more attractive than mine. I was self-conscious and a little embarrassed to follow them; I was not as fit as I had been in my youth.

I watched them walk into the spring before I took off the rest of my clothes. I was struck by the rose tattoo at the base of Juanita's spine, reminded again that no encounter ever occurs by accident. The tattoo reminded me of April and the digging of clay in the Arizona desert. I savored this reminder of certainty about daily existence that I had not fully grasped before this. This made it easier for me to dispatch with the rest of my clothes.

My silly and immature reservations about being naked vanished. Before long, I reached the edge of the water. It was very hot, and I was more than a little sensitive to the temperature as I slowly eased my entire body into the water. The heat moved through me; the warmth penetrated every muscle, and it felt good. The heat moving through me felt like a current, a plane that could take my spirit anywhere it wanted to go. Pedro must have had a pretty good idea about what I was thinking.

He asked me, "Where does it take you? Where does it take you, Dolmen?"

"Far, far away," I said.

I felt my spirit being lifted up to a very high mountain. From there I saw me. I was so small from up there. I thought that when I was down below there, how much bigger I actually must have truly been. Appearances were deceiving and gave many wrong impressions. How could I be any different whether I was lying in the stream or standing on top of the mountain? How could this be?

Juanita said the *balnearios* made us see the world of appearances differently, including our own appearances. She described a similar experience that happened to her, saying that after the experience, she felt connected to water and the earth. She stopped feeling the boundary between her skin and the water. Exterior became interior, interior became exterior.

I think the part of me that Medir had encouraged me to honor understood what she was saying, though I don't now recall exactly what she said. Being naked in the spring, I didn't exactly have a place to carry a pen and paper to write it down for later consideration!

What I do remember is how I felt so peaceful and so safe with these two people. I had only just met them a few days ago, yet I felt so alive and connected to what they were saying. Being naked was no longer a cause for fear or shame. The water created a powerful bond between us. I felt a familiarity with them, as if they were my own children. I wondered if this happened to all who entered these springs.

Sometimes fewer words speak more clearly. This was certainly true when it came to surrendering to the consciousness of this present moment. I could not add anything useful to what Juanita and Pedro had already said by adding my own silly comments. They were speaking truths, and my soul was being stirred and awakened by the waters. I was tuned to their words and carried by an invisible force to the center of this sacred place. In this moment I felt a complete and total unity with them and my surroundings. All of our ears were tuned to the deep bass resonance that must have been the hum of the Great Unseen. Bi would probably say we were listening to MIRRI. It was an illusion to think that any of us could ever be separate.

"It is time for us to get out of the water before we melt into jelly!" Pedro laughed. "Come over here."

I followed them a short distance to a muddy bank, where they picked up the mud and smeared it on themselves. I followed their example, scooping up the sulfur-smelling mud with my hands and completely covering my body with it. Pedro and Juanita helped each other cover themselves with the mud, going over the spots that they could not reach without help. Pedro did the same for me.

We moved a few feet to a sandy spot where an opening through the trees allowed the sun to shine through. The three of us lay down, eyes closed, saying nothing. We were surrounded by the sound of the water, the magic of the sun, the bond of this space that held us together like the creatures God had fashioned from the earth. We were in sync with each other as by some invisible mechanism. The mud dried like plaster casts to our skin.

I thought of the pots that I'd made back home. I thought about Hekeke rescuing Pen and me in the desert the time we ran out of gas. I thought about him leading us to the clay. I thought about Medir's welcome and how Pedro and Juanita were instruments of divine healing, helping me to be reformed and remade. I was a new pot in the making.

Pedro and Juanita stood up, and I followed their example. It was time for us to go to the falls. Fresh water from the falls removed the mud from our skin. My shyness had also left me. I no longer worried about any physical inadequacies, imagined or otherwise, as we helped each other remove the remnants of the clay from places that were hard to see or reach. Innocence, purity, beauty, transformation, and rejuvenation are all words that describe how I was feeling.

This is what I remember from my time at the springs: I felt the playfulness of being a child again. I felt like I had just come out of my shell. The EBK Travel Agency staff had cracked open the egg of an entity that was not totally captured by the name Dolmen, and a new being, a new life was being hatched. In our nakedness, the three of us walked back to our clothes. We were naked, but not afraid.

The sun had moved lower in the sky. As we walked back to fetch our clothes, I saw it frame the table-like structures of the rock. We dressed and got back up on our horses to begin the journey home. No words were necessary, for everything had been said and experienced. This was not a time for more words or questions. It felt like I was leaving a sanctuary with the quiet and reverence of someone who'd just received the Eucharist from an invisible priest.

I knew that after this time together, Pedro and Juanita would always be a part of my family. I felt the same way about Medir. I knew this was obvious to them, too, although they had no need to verbalize this bond because they already knew it and lived it.

We returned to the camp we'd used the previous day and spent the night. After a night of deep and restful sleep, we made the rest of the trip back to Medir's home.

I looked forward to seeing her and sharing my experience at the *balnearios*. The evening after we returned, she joined me. I felt close to Medir and found that it required no effort to trust her.

When I saw Medir, I said, "You were right. You didn't need to tell me about what I would find there. The words are only an approximation for the experience."

Medir said, "I am happy to talk with you, because you see now, in a new way, that we are family…Yes, that we are *all* family. We have always been family, originating from the same place. It is not a place that is visible to the eyes, only to the heart. Before, with your busy corporate life, you would not have understood or imagined how we could be in the same place—this place is so far away from your home and all of the routines—but now you know it, too, is only an appearance. It is a mirage. It is not real.

"The *balnearios* opened your eyes to the fact that your home is here, too. It is everywhere and nowhere, on the mountain or in the river; it makes no difference where you are, although everything can look so different, so exciting. Did looking at the mountain make it higher or lower? Did it make you bigger or smaller?

"Now you feel you have come home, even though you are thousands of miles from where you have always told others you live. Home is not a place. It has no address, unless you have a description for such a place that cannot be seen or driven to.

"Without the healing powers of the water, you would still believe that you could tell the difference between what is important and what is not, what something appears to be and what the truth is beyond all appearances. You needed to be helped by the gift of the waters to see things differently. It is harder to let go of your ideas about what is real and what is not than it is to take off your clothes and expose your body to strangers. The waters helped you to remove things that hold you back, which is more important than what you wear to conceal what seems important, but does not matter in the least."

"Yes," I said. "I know something has happened, and it will take me some time to take it all in."

She continued, "Now you know the reason I stay here, even though my husband is gone. This is my place. This is where I am supposed to be. This will be my place for as long as I'm here. From here I send my intention, aligning myself with all who will come here.

"It is not a matter of when the people come to this place. Think of your first dinner here; many guests joined you at the table. We were all together in the moment. Whether they were here years ago or will be making the trip to the *balnearios* at some later time, it doesn't really matter. When you were in the water, you did not care about anything in the past or worry about anything in the future; that is how it can feel when we stop allowing ourselves to be controlled by limiting beliefs about the past or fears about the future. When I walk around the ranch doing my daily activities, I do not feel I ever left the *balnearios*. I don't need to travel anywhere in the world. I live here, but do not live here. I am in the world that people think is real, but I am a resident in a land that no one can see. Señor Ebkilfgn helps all who come here to find their true home. The *balnearios* that you visited are inside of me, inside the vessels that hold my blood, inside my being. It is not possible to find words to describe it."

I stayed at the ranch for a couple more days, pondering what had happened. I thought about all the things Medir said to me. It felt like parts of me that were so easily fractured before by stress were becoming more coherent. I was like a pot that had lacked the proper combination of clay and other materials to balance the need for elasticity, permanence, and the solidity to hold together had finally taken shape after being fired. I was eager to see Pen and tell her what had happened. I amused myself by thinking that I should be really grateful for Pen's three-month extension. How was that for a new spin on my current situation?

I wondered if this was happening to Pen, too. My sense of family, of kinship, exceeded any previous understanding of the notion. I now considered Medir, Pedro, and Juanita as a part of my family, and it was easy to imagine others like April or Beki in the same way. Also, what about Pablo, Calde, and Elle? Were they not also a part of a much larger family, one that I simply did not know about until very recently?

Established appearances dissolved like the waters that flowed through me to leave a shared inner core that I could not explain, but I felt. Though I was thousands of miles away from my wife and children, I felt a closeness to them that was not simply personal or familial. It was no accident that they were my family and that my awareness of who or what I might consider family was changing. Contrary to appearances, I felt closer to my dear Penelope at that moment than I ever had, although I missed her very much and she was miles away.

When it was nearly time for me to fly back to the states, Medir asked, "Could we have dinner tomorrow, Dolmen? I know it is getting close to your time to leave us."

"Yes, of course. I would love to do that."

After dinner the following evening, Medir said, "Your time here is nearly over. I want to speak with you about something."

"And what is that?"

Medir answered, "You were the sign that she was waiting for."

"Who was waiting for?"

"Juanita. I want you to take her with you."

"What? What do you mean?"

"I cannot explain, but I know it. I feel it. Juanita has said similar things to me. Talk with her. Take her with you, back to your country. She is ready to continue her journey, and that journey is with your family in the United States."

"You mean our family," I teased her.

Medir smiled and said, "Yes, Dolmen, with *our* family."

After some discussion, I agreed to take Juanita with me.

Soon it was time to say goodbye to Medir. I would miss her and the ranch. Pedro brought us to the airport. I sat silently, wondering if I would ever see them again. Juanita was my travelling partner, which would take Degen by surprise. We hugged Pedro and began the rest of the journey back to the States.

When we got off the plane, Degen was there, and sure enough, he was not expecting another passenger. I introduced him to Juanita and explained that I would provide her with a place to stay until she found employment and got on her feet.

Degen drove us back home and spent the night with us. Juanita stayed in the guest bedroom.

Degen seemed a bit shell-shocked. He said, "Is everything okay, Dad? You look a little different. Are you sure you are feeling okay?"

I reassured Degen. I told him that I was actually feeling better at that moment than I had in my entire life.

Degen said, "I don't know what happened over there. I can't really explain how you seem different, but I guess that vacation must have been exactly what you needed."

It was true. I returned home with a greater sense of peace about the new direction of my life.

Soon the remaining days of Pen's three-month extension had elapsed. It was finally time to pick up the information and make my travel arrangements for Tibet.

On the appointed day, I returned to the building. Nothing had changed. There was no sign of the instructor or the posters for the class. I went in and recognized the same security guard from three months ago. He recognized me, and we made small talk. He was funny and ironic.

Then he said to me, "Sir, I think we could set our clocks and calendars by your timeliness. They told me that you would be here this morning at 9:00 a.m., and here you are."

He handed me the envelope and said, "This is what you have been waiting for. Have a good day."

"And you do the same," I said.

This time I did not rush to the coffee shop to tear open the envelope. I drove home thinking that whatever might be in the envelope would be fine with me; it was just another step. Though I did not wish for another three-month time extension, even that would have been okay.

When I opened the envelope, I was happy to find out that there would be no further delay. All of the details for my trip were included: A flight itinerary, the name of a hotel, and a contact person. I was excited and energized by the thought that soon I would be heading to Tibet to be reunited with my dear Penelope.

## CHAPTER 8

# *TIBET REVISITED*

I was excited to share the news with Degen that I would soon be heading to Tibet, and in turn found out that he'd helped Juanita find a job with an IT firm.

Soon I was on the plane that would reunite me with Pen. It was a long flight followed by a taxi to the hotel. A message at the desk told me that my contact would meet me in the morning.

That night I fell asleep and had a dream about a shimmering lake.

*I walk to the edge and sit down on a bench. An Asian woman sits down next to me and removes a small pouch from her basket. She opens the pouch and empties it. It contains three round, clear stones. She throws the first stone into the water and I watch circles of water form from the stone's welcome. The welcome grows with each moment, so many circles surrounding each other. It is an applause that moves further and further from the initial welcome until all is quiet. She throws the second stone into the water. When it touches the surface of the water, the stone splits into twelve more stones that scatter in equal directions before falling to the bottom; now there are twelve patterns. Twelve welcomes occur spontaneously and in harmony with each other, all welcoming the twelve stones. When these patterns cross, the lines in the water turn into the vines of plants. Then she tosses the third stone into the middle of this cluster of vines. At first I don't see another welcome from the water, but then a Lotus flower unfolds in the center, where she had cast the last stone. She smiles at me, her eyes looking like two pearls, and then she walks away.*

*I get up and walk to the edge of the water. Taking off my shoes and socks, I wade into the water to look at the flower more closely. The water is crystal clear, but when I look into it, I cannot see my legs or my feet even though I can clearly see the bottom of the pond through the clear water. I am nearly to the vines and the flower when a slender fish with beautiful rainbow markings on its side swims toward me. At just the instant I sense it would bump into my legs, I feel nothing. The fish swims below me, occupying the space where my legs and feet should have been. I panic and try even harder to feel my legs and feet beneath me, holding me up, but I feel no sensation in them at all. When I reach into the water to feel them, I only feel the body of the fish. When I pull my hand out of the water, something round and solid sits in the palm of my hand. I think it is a stone, but when I look at it I know the fish gave me a pearl. I look into the water again, and now I can see my feet. I look for the fish, but it was gone.*

The next morning, I met the young man who would bring me to Pen. It was not Pen's teacher, but he reminded me of him. He took me by car out of the noisy city and to the grounds of a monastery. There were flowers, shrines, stones, trees, and ponds. The grounds were beautiful, and they were breathing peace. The driver introduced me to my host and then the master's assistant. Her name was Loux Han. I asked her if she knew Pen and if Pen had completed her apprenticeship.

Loux Han said, "Yes, I know her very well. It has been a great honor to be with her."

"Is she finished with her training?"

Loux Han replied, "In a manner of speaking, yes. She is finished here."

We walked the grounds of the monastery and continued to talk about Pen.

"She has learned much by letting go of much, and I can see that you are learning very much the same in your own way, yes?"

When Loux Han smiled at me, I felt her radiance and warmth. It felt like the shimmer of light on the surface of a lake. Her hair was silver, and she wore a small ornament in her hair that bore all the colors of the rainbow.

She continued before I had answered her. "She has learned to paint with her heart and let it guide her brush, but the brush is also a symbol for the daily actions taken when painting on our personal canvas."

"What do you mean?" I asked.

"When you choose to take a walk, that walk is one stroke of the brush; buying a new car or some other item is another stroke of the brush on your canvas. Singing a song is still another stroke of the brush. Accumulating many things takes many more brush strokes. Do you see what I mean?"

She continued. "One must know when to stroke and where to place the next stroke of the brush upon the canvas." She pointed to a flower near us. "Look at the Lotus flower. It is a lovely flower that was created with an invisible brush of the Spirit. No single word can describe its beauty or essence because its essence lies beyond human perception. The intelligence of the Great Unseen fashioned it with one perfect stroke. What follows is just a manifestation of what was done beyond time and space. The invisible stroke of the Creator made it obvious which stroke must follow the next, and the next, until all that follows was needed. Eventually you and I can see the results. It is beautiful. If we could imagine ourselves to be inside of every petal, each stroke would be obvious."

I asked, "How does one know where to start painting? I don't understand what it is that Pen learned here."

Loux Han replied, "The answer to this question is found within oneself. I cannot explain this to you. Penelope has become attuned to the invisible stroke of the Creator through her daily work on the mountain.

"Your wife has learned that the true Painter lies within her, just as the true beauty of the Lotus flower is only appreciated from the inside. Its beauty lies within. Most people, of course, do not consider or understand such things. To them, it is just one more flower. Now, her painting expresses even more than what can be easily seen. Painting always manifests what is hidden. Penelope has learned to hold her brush by letting go of trying to control it, by surrendering herself. Now every stroke that she makes originates in her heart."

There was a long pause in our conversation, and then Loux Han said, "Penelope will return from her cabin tomorrow."

"Where is the cabin?"

Loux Han pointed in the direction of a vast mountain range. "It is a long way, but she will be here tomorrow. She has been headed in our direction for several days. You are free to wander about. Make yourself comfortable."

She showed me to my room and told me where and when I could find tea and rice.

I took Loux Han's advice and strolled around the beautiful grounds. I looked at the flowers, trying to see them from the inside out. I was not able to discern the difference, although I think I understood what she said to me. Since her training, I wondered what Pen saw when she looked at a flower. I wondered if I would be able to see the difference in her paintings. Mostly, I was so excited to finally see her again.

Before my conversation with Loux Han, I was eager to share my stories with Pen. After that conversation, I was more eager to listen to her. I thought of how self-absorbed I had been about my interests and discoveries. Pen had accompanied me on all of my trips without hesitation or objection, every step of the way. I was beginning to realize that my canvas was no more important or interesting than hers—or anyone else's, for that matter.

Pen arrived through the front gate as promised the following afternoon. There were no more delays or time extensions. She was wearing clothes and sandals unlike anything I had seen her wear before. As she walked toward me, I was struck by her balance, her poise, and her serenity. The word "countenance" came into my mind as I tried to understand what I was seeing when I looked at her face. She looked slender, almost too slender. She looked so much thinner than I had ever seen her, but she did not look sick. She looked peaceful.

"Hello, Dolmen," she said. "I'm so glad to see you. I've missed you. I love you."

"I'm so glad to see you. I love you. I've missed you, too."

There were tears in her eyes; they triggered my own, which were just waiting for the right moment to surface.

"My Pen," I said. "My dearest Penelope, I love you. I love you. I missed you so much."

We kissed and embraced for a long time. It felt so good to hold her.

Loux Han arranged a simple and private meal in a nearby cottage. We shared tea, rice, and stories.

It is hard to describe what it was like to be with Pen again. I knew that both of us had many things to share, which we would do in the days and months ahead. They would come out in their own appointed time. I didn't feel any rush. I felt a quiet exhilaration. I breathed easier; if I'd had any fears about her return, these seemed to have vanished.

*Yes,* I told myself, *I will simply enjoy the gift of Pen's presence.* That day, just being together, that was enough. Perhaps it could be attributed to the significant length of our separation, but I felt that day had birthed a new attentiveness between us. I was warmed by the thought and hope that Pen felt the same way.

As promised, the itinerary gave us thirty days in Tibet before we needed to return home. This was welcomed as time for us to catch up with each other. I had believed that so much had happened to me that was not obvious from the outside, and Loux Han's words spoke insightfully and clearly about what was happening inside Pen.

"Dolmen, I can tell that you have much to tell me," Pen started. "I want to hear all about it."

"How do you know?"

"Because you are different."

"That's true. I am, and it's not just about the pottery."

"I know. I can feel it."

"And you? This trip is not just about the painting."

"Yes, I have learned much about myself. I, too, am a different person."

I told her that I wanted her to show me her work and explain it to me, and she agreed to do just that.

I knew that the month together would pass quickly as we brought each other up to speed as much as we could about the recent events in her life and mine. I was a work in progress, an uncompleted project. I was eager to learn of the changes that had taken place for her.

She said that there was a tradition among the local people that when loved ones were reunited after a long absence, it was good luck to bring a gift.

"What kind of gift?" I asked.

"Something that speaks to the moment of being together again."

Pen reached into a small purse to remove something and put it in the palm of my hand.

"Hold it up to the light and let the sun see it. Tell me what you see."

I did as she asked, holding the object, a small stone, up in the air so that it faced the sun. I saw all the colors of the rainbow dancing inside the stone.

"It's beautiful. Where did you find it?"

"I found it on one of my walks on the mountain. Maybe it found me. It is for you. It is an expression of my love and belief in you."

I lowered my hand, feeling the contours of the stone.

Pen continued. "Each night I held it in my hand as I said my prayers, keeping it in my hand through the night. I thought about you, wishing you joy, safety, and peace."

The stone felt warm in my hand. I felt my body relax as I held it.

"What is in this rock? I feel something when I hold it. I feel relaxed, peaceful."

Pen replied, "It holds my intention to love you without conditions, expectations, or grievances."

Something about the stone reminded me of the third stone in my dream. Pen saw my reaction to her gift and smiled. I told her it was a beautiful gift that I would treasure and that from this day forward, I would always carry it in my pocket. I hesitated to say more because I needed time to think about what was happening to me.

It seemed like another one of those moments in which one should appreciate the power and beauty of restraint, trusting that it is not always necessary to spew all of what we think we know about something. I kept back the vanity of my opinions and the need to make an editorial comment about anything that popped into my head. For that moment, it was best to just silently enjoy the beautiful and simple gift. The beautiful flowers and the trees behind Pen diffracted the sunlight, so I told her how beautiful she looked, but I thought of the fish with the rainbow markings.

Could Pen know from some place that she'd discovered in herself that this stone would be so meaningful or create such a powerful response in me? I had not thought it possible that the simple act of holding a stone each night could communicate her love for me so clearly. I wondered if it might be possible that my pots could also do such things. Could pottery be made into containers of intention? How could pottery do this?

I started to say a few words about this, forgetting the resolution not to do so I'd made less than a minute ago, but then decided it was not the time. Later I would share with her my dreams and the real-life experiences that seemed to replay them in a different but recognizable form. I would share this newfound ability to let the meaning of my dream reveal itself with her at the appointed and proper time. I learned this in the *balnearios* in Spain, and I hoped that I would never forget the sense of awe and completion I'd had when I did not feel the water because I had become the water.

Pen and I made the journey to the cabin she'd stayed at on foot with a mule and some provisions. There was no escort, guard, or guide to ensure our safety. Pen didn't seem the least bit worried or nervous.

"It's all right, darling. Trust me, this journey is a good way for us to get to know one another again and bring everything in our relationship into its proper place."

The cabin took one week to reach on foot. We stayed overnight in tiny villages along the way. People recognized Pen. I felt their affection for her and her affection for them. She told me about the Chinese and how they had done so much harm to the people in Tibet. She told me that Tibetan prayers were for healing the whole world, including their oppressors.

Finally, we made it to the cabin. I saw where she painted, meditated, and did her exercises. We walked in the alpine meadows where she had been inspired to use her brush in new ways to express the essence of flowers. This was not like the hiking we'd done with the kids. She moved differently as she walked these paths and told me about the past six months.

We returned to the monastery for the last few days and then it was time to go home.

At the end of the trip, I had a much better sense of both the serenity and magic of Tibet and the peacefulness that seemed to radiate from within Penelope.

When we arrived home, we learned that our son and Juanita were more than friends. They intended to be married. How strange life could be! Pen and I were both happy for Degen. I smiled from the inside out thinking of Medir's request to bring Juanita with me. I thanked the Great Unseen (or was it MIRRI?) for giving me another sign.

Things looked like they were back to normal, though much had changed for both of us. I tried to make pots from the heart and with intention, which required not a new technical skill but a way of visualizing from within. I tried to return to the feelings I had when I felt so formless in the water, cleansed by the mud and rebirthed by its removal to be a new person. I thought about myself as a clay vessel, that the clay simply contained or held me. I realized that though it appeared I was made of clay, *I really wasn't the clay*. The clay was just a temporary container for me. I was being carried by the pot, somehow living inside the pot. I thought about my dream of being in the water with my legs no longer visible to me.

I wondered where the illusion was. Was it the certainty of seeing my legs and being reassured by touching them? Was the truth completely invisible to my senses, hidden within the water? Was the truth somehow carried within the pot?

Before the trip to Argentina that awakened me to what the professor had told me long ago, none of these thoughts would have occurred to a numbers guy, a bean counter like me. If it had not been for the seemingly unplanned, yet somehow completely orchestrated events of my life, I would still be stuck at the office. I was learning how to think and experience life differently. I was being remade by the water, the clay, the dreams, and especially the people who came into my life in so many unexpected ways. I was no longer a believer in coincidence, statistics, or probabilities. The numbers guy was trying to let himself be guided by something that he had been told was foolish, impulsive, and possibly dangerous.

My thoughts took me further away from my office. Who needed a plane to do that? None of these events were the result of studying a new book or taking a business class. The most critical decisions of my life couldn't be made by a yes vote from a board of directors or by reading between the lines of the financial pages for clues. I realized that my previously rock-solid way of going through life was a faulty belief system and was equally guilty of the charge of silliness. It was faulty because it was so rigid, so narrow, so small.

I came to believe that a plan was unfolding in my life from the inside out by the power of MIRRI, the Great Unseen, the Great Spirit, God—it didn't really matter what I called it, since it was all divine. It was the manifestation of the consciousness of the author of my life. My canvas was being painted by every intention, every thought and feeling I had. These strokes would expand or shrink my canvas, and while it was my doing, I was not alone and it was more than just my own doing. I struggled for words to describe what I meant using imprecise, unmathematical language. While the brush and canvas were Pen's tools of transformation, mine was clay, and that suited me fine. I was pleased to be working with the clay because I knew that it was not about the medium. We shared a common catalyst, the only true catalyst—intention.

Even though my pots lacked the finality or security of a completed report at the office, I felt a kind of peace about my life when my hands were covered with clay. Pen could tell, and that made her happy. I sensed that Degen and Juanita also knew this about me. That felt good. If I had followed the safe routes and not taken any risks, I would still be spending my extra time after work accumulating stuff and letting life pass me by.

I would be clueless and numb, not knowing the difference between what is true or false or what is real or not. I would not know where a particular boundary begins or when one has passed beyond it. I had a growing sense that I was learning more about the bowl the professor gave me to hold all those years ago. I was hopeful that I was on the way to learning more about that hunk of clay, that particular pot called Dolmen.

I was certain that something was unfolding. The pots that I started to fashion at this stage did not look particularly different, but I thought more about the space inside the pots. I thought they felt different when I held them with this thought in mind. I wondered how this could be. How could my focus change the feeling I had when I held the pot? While I knew my experiences were changing me and propelling me forward, I had not acquired any new technical skill in my touch, in my experiences, or through my travels. I do know that I was evolving to a different level of understanding. Perhaps my pots would acquire the quality of the stone that Pen had held for so many nights on the mountain.

My world was getting better. It was changing from the inside out through the power of intention. While Dolmen was still the man who lived at this address and worked in his potting shed, there was something or someone else living inside Dolmen, and the address of this entity was not the same as mine—or was it that I had many addresses? I saw my home and its physical structure as an incomplete description of my real address. I was both here and someplace else. It was like the experience in Spain of being both smaller and bigger at the same time depending on where you were sitting. Yes, I thought, this was not the only place that I lived. You could find me all over the world, separated only by the veil of appearances. I lived in a much larger community. I was a resident of a much bigger place. I thought of Tibet, Spain, Mozambique, Argentina, and Arizona as I thought about my larger address. I thought there were probably still more places that I could call home. *Yes, Dolmen*, I said to myself, *you are all over the world.* I felt that my home was much larger and that my studio resided in every one of these places. Although I couldn't put what I was trying to express into words, my intuition told me that I was living in twelve places at the same time.

I decided that this must be what it meant to have moved to a higher level of consciousness. I knew that I felt less driven, less separate, and less desperate. I was becoming more courageous about doing what was in my heart and being open to purposes unfolding within me. The events of my life were an invitation to see everything differently. I was softer, more compassionate, and more peaceful.

My hands moved without thinking as they worked quickly in crafting pots. I only thought about the space that was being created inside the pots; the pottery simply defined boundaries in some way. I believed that every human being occupied such a pot, that all of us must have our own messages to listen to—he who has ears to hear, let him hear.

It was important to pay intention to what was inside and to not pay as much attention to the particular shape or appearance of the pot. What mattered was what the pot held. If we could remember this, eventually we would be able to surrender all of the excuses that surface within ourselves when we think we have no choice or voice. I found it more and more difficult to think that the answer to the questions of my life, or any person's life, for that matter, could be explained by bad luck or circumstance.

I felt hopeful. I knew that it was up to only me to awaken to the notion that there is a time and place for everything. I wondered if the same experiences that were propelling my life forward were available to everyone. I knew that the answer must be yes as clearly as I knew Bi lifted that fish out of the water for everyone to be fed. I wondered how many times human beings had refused the invitation to gain a deeper understanding of themselves. It would make no sense if only a few us had the opportunity to experience these things.

I also thought that it was an illusion to think it was me who fashioned any pot, especially if I thought from the inside out. The thing that brought the clay together and held it in place was invisible, hidden within the clay. The power of my intention was my only contribution. This was very important, even critical to moving forward, but it was only a small part. I appreciated how I learned to cooperate with the clay, to align myself with it, and to interact with its inherent energies and spirit.

# CHAPTER 9
## *ECUADOR*

It was at about this time that I experienced another powerful dream.

*I am inside the pot. The interior walls tell the stories of my life and show its pictures. The inside is smooth. The walls are like a screen upon which the movie of my life is being played. I feel as though I am in a cave. It begins to rain and the water inside begins to rise. My legs disappear again; soon the rising water level has reached my chest and everything below my chest has disappeared. I feel the cave itself being lifted and turned over. I feel myself being carried by the water out of the opening; I am being poured out. I see a girl's face above me. From below the surface of the water, I can tell that she is scooping me up with her hands. I feel myself scattered across her face. I am gliding down her neck and landing in a pocket of flesh above her clavicle. I see a row of amethyst stones on the surface of her skin. She is refreshed by the water...Or is it me? Am I the water? In the distance I hear the sound of a quetzal.*

The figure of the bird stays with me as I wake up.

Lying in bed, trying to hold onto the dream, I realized that the amethysts were a sign of where I would be going next. I expected the answer to appear soon. I closed my eyes again, trying to let the water from my dream cover me again. I wanted to peer through the water to see her face, but it was morning and I was too awake.

A couple of days later, Pen and I took a stroll around a nearby lake. A woman walked past us on her way to the playground with her children. I noticed a bracelet on her wrist that contained a string of amethysts, and I listened to my intuition and decided to approach her and ask about the bracelet.

"That is a beautiful bracelet. I was wondering where you purchased it."

"Last summer at an art fair," she said.

She told me about where the art fair had been held, and I thanked her for the information.

When I contacted the people who ran the fair, I was able to obtain a list of the exhibitors, which included the name of the person who sold amethyst jewelry. When Pen and I went to see her, she told us the stones came from Ecuador. We asked about how she obtained the jewelry she sold, which lead to us doing more sleuthing. Eventually we traced our way through the buyers and sellers to the original importer.

The woman who imported the amethysts lived several hours away from us, but I was determined to meet her so we made the trip. We found her office and I introduced myself to her.

I told her about how much I liked the amethysts in the jewelry that came from Ecuador and asked if it would be possible to go and see where the stones were mined.

"Yes, of course," she replied. "It is possible, but anything you need we can make here."

She continued. "It is not customary for outsiders to go to that mine. It is a long way and in very remote area of the country. The road can be treacherous, and it will cost you a lot of money to go on your own. It would be much more economical for you to wait until we receive more stones. I will make sure you get a very high quality stone, and I'm sure we can make anything you would like."

I replied, "Thanks very much for your willingness to do that for me, but I would like to see it for myself and meet the people who find them."

"Very well, it can be arranged. It's your money, your life, and your adventure, right?"

She was surprised, but not offended. Maybe she was also intrigued or amused by my desire to go there.

Pen agreed to fly with me to Ecuador. It was a long flight to Quito. After three more days of travel, we were in a small town on the edge of a region that was not exactly a tourist attraction. Not knowing what else to do, I gave the name of the importer to the owner of the only hotel in the town. She recognized her name and said that she visited the town on rare occasions. When she asked why I did not wait at home for more stones to arrive, I could only think about my dream. She smiled at me much like the importer back in the States did.

I said nothing more about it, but she looked at me with what felt like more than curiosity. It was an unexpected surprise when she said that she was pleased we had come to her town. She added that she would be very happy to make the rest of the arrangements to get me to the mine.

She finished with, "If your wife would like to stay here and paint, she will find more than enough to fill her imagination and her canvases."

We had said nothing to her that would have suggested that Pen was a painter. How could she possibly have known? It wasn't like the word "painter" was written on Pen's forehead!

Pen said, "That is very kind of you. I would be happy to do just that while Dolmen is gone."

Pen then turned to me and simply said, "Yes, I know it is a sign, Dolmen. I know that you need to go." Pen spoke with a sincerity that left no question in my mind about going to the mine and leaving her alone at the hotel.

That evening I considered once more that what I was learning to hold in my mind would reveal itself when the time was right. This thought ensured a night of peaceful sleep.

The next morning, I said goodbye to Pen. "I'll see you when I get back. Don't worry, I won't be long, darling."

Pen said the best words to me. She said, "I'll be there with you." I thought of the stone she gave me in Tibet.

I told Pen, "Yes, I know. I feel that way, too."

With that, my guide led me out of the town and toward a pass between two mountains. He said our destination was just beyond what was only a spot on the horizon on the other side of the mountain.

Our destination was a tiny village, where one of the villagers met us at the entrance. My guide was known to them. The villager greeted us, but I did not understand their language.

The guide translated to English for me. "He is surprised and not certain why you are here."

I looked at the villager, gazing into his eyes. Then I reached out and grabbed both of his hands. I visualized the girl from my dream with the amethyst stones.

A moment later, he spoke to my guide.

The guide turned to me and translated. "We have been expecting you. Welcome to our home. Tomorrow, I will bring you to the place you want to see."

The next morning, my guide and the man who welcomed us led the way out of the village and into the jungle. We followed a path for a few miles that eventually brought us to the edge of a river that flowed past the mountain.

There were a few people standing at the edge of the river. Others moved in and out of the mountain carrying pails of rocks. We walked to the river, and I could feel that familiar surge of power. I thought of the hum, the deep bass voice that I experienced at the *balnearios*. I was certain that I would soon see the woman from my last dream, and I was not disappointed. I spotted her. In a remote location in a far-away country called Ecuador, a place that had never been on my bucket list to visit, there she was.

I knew it was her. She was crouched along the bank of the river, surrounded by a few villagers listening to her instructions. She held a sieve in her hands, which the villagers emptied a pail of rocks into. She added water and mud to the rocks and slowly shook the sieve to separate the contents, and then she used her hands to further sift the material. This was how she examined and sorted everything that was taken out of the mountain.

In my heart, I knew that it was her. I saw the necklace made of amethyst. She looked up and saw me. I believe that she must have had her own dream about a stranger coming to Ecuador from an unknown place. My guide told me that her name was Nemea and that she was a descendant of the Incas.

I observed the process of digging and mining and then refining and separating what was taken from the mountain. She showed the villagers where to use their picks in the mountain caves to find the precious stones, and they brought the broken rocks to her for the final sorting. Much of what she identified was given to others and presumably went on for commercial processing so they would find their way into many cities throughout the world as finished merchandise—some deemed suitable for high-end jewelry stores and other pieces for art fairs, where the prices were not so high. The string of amethysts decorating the bracelet worn by the woman in our town originated in this mine, with Nemea telling the others where to find them in the mountain and separating them into a pile to send thousands of miles away.

Nemea also set aside a small pile of stones that she would fashion for other purposes for her village. I was sure that it was from a pile like this that her necklace was made. She gave the pile she'd separated from the others to a man who placed them in a barrel with some clay and water. That went into another barrel that would turn the rocks over and over again for many weeks. After watching this, my guide told me that it was time to return to the village, telling me that according to the village elder, I was welcome to stay in the village for as long as I'd like.

The only person who spoke any English was my guide. He explained to me that I was Nemea's expected guest and that I was welcome in their village. He told me that I would join her at the river every day that I was there and that I would eat with Nemea and sleep next to her in her hut. There was something quite magical about being around Nemea. She would fashion a stone into the jewel that I came for.

"Is she making me a bracelet or a necklace?" I asked.

The guide said, "I don't think so."

At the river the next day, one of the men was bitten on the ankle by a poisonous snake. One of the others rushed to find Nemea and quickly explained what had happened. She motioned for me to follow her into the jungle, so I did. She dug up an unfamiliar-looking plant with a knife and we hurried back to the river. She cut the roots off the plant and put the roots into a bowl. She poured water over the roots and ground them into a paste while singing something that I did not understand. Then she submerged her hands into the river, as had happened in my dream. Nemea scooped up the paste and rubbed it into the man's wounds, speaking words that I did not understand. His friends helped him back to the village. The next day, the poisonous snake bite was healed.

That night I lay next to Nemea in her hut and held her hands. Soon I felt like I was back in the river in Spain. Then Nemea spoke, using more words that I did not understand, and I felt a surge of energy through me. I felt like I was on top of the mountain. I was so high that everything below me was too tiny for me to know what it was. I felt like I was experiencing some kind of deeper unity and resonance within me. I was aware of the oneness that encompassed all things in creation. This oneness transcended male or female; animal, human, or plant; animate or inanimate; real or virtual. Then she uttered a single word: Huhahe.

The next morning, I asked my guide what the word meant.

He said, "There is no word for this in your language—God, maybe."

Two more days passed before my guide informed me that what I'd come for was completed.

"Nemea will give it to you this evening," he said.

As we lay in the hut beside each other that night, a small tool rested on the ground between us. The tool was attached to a simple necklace, and I thought it was a tool used to inscribe and decorate pottery.

I thanked her for the gift, and she smiled and said only one word, which she never uttered again to me. She said, "Ebkilfgn."

The next morning I asked my guide to find out more about the gift she gave me, and the guide confirmed that it was an inscribing tool.

Then he explained, "But your tool is to be worn around your neck as a good luck charm. Nemea knows that you are a potter even though you never told her, but your tool is not to be used to mark your pots. You are supposed to wear it."

The next day we headed back to town. Before we left, the village elder came to see me. As I stood before him, he extended his hand placed it over my chest, on top of the tool. He smiled at me and said, "Huhahe."

As I walked back to the hotel, I thought about what had happened with Nemea and about the gift. It was a tool for inscribing jewelry or other precious articles, like my pots, but this was meant as a symbolic tool and not something to be used back in my potting shed. I realized that the true inscription of my pots would not come from external marks etched into their surfaces. True inscription would come from within, just as it was for Pen and her painting. Intent shapes the interior of the vessel from the inside out, not the other way around. The gift from Nemea would help remind me that I was seeking to be guided by intent, that intent was inscribing the contours of my life. My most important task was to let go of my fears and keep trusting that I was fulfilling my purpose. To know this within my soul was to know Huhahe. Like MIRRI, it was a sacred word.

There is a unity that exists beyond any physical separation I could possibly imagine. In this remote village, Nemea recognized me. She knew me in a way that did not rely on the usual ways of learning about other people. The tool she made me was proof that there is a universal field of information that does not require a common spoken language.

I believe my dreams, travels, and encounters helped me to appreciate this vast field of information, this invisible library that carried the answers to any question one might imagine. Then I thought that besides the tool, there was another gift that Huhahe gave Nemea to share with me: A word. It was a word that I still did not understand, but one that connected me to a man I met once—the professor. This man was apparently known by people throughout the world who lacked any obvious connection between them.

Ebkilfgn. When Nemea uttered this single word, I felt that I was awakening to a higher purpose. I realized that I hadn't any idea where I had really come from. I felt that I was a representative of a race that could not be described as American, African, Asian, or European. Who exactly am I? What is humanity's common link, our common origin? What has this to do with Ebkilfgn?

When my guide and I got back to the hotel, I greeted Pen. She had enjoyed the painting and her new friendship with the owner of the hotel. When Pen looked at me, I knew that she could tell I'd found what I was after.

It was time to return home.

# CHAPTER 10

# *JAPAN*

One day Degen and Juanita called to tell us they'd accepted an offer to move to Japan. They had become a successful professional team—Juanita had developed a novel IT application that processed volumes of genetic data according to a new paradigm that had significant impact for energy production, and this magnified and accelerated Degen's experiments. This helped to spark the new project with the Japanese firm.

One year later, they invited us to visit, and Pen and I received an invitation to have dinner with the company's CEO, a Japanese man in his eighties. His name was Hue Yamakazi.

"I've heard much about you," he said. "I am most glad that you have come."

I felt that unmistakable familiar feeling when I shook his hand.

"Your son and daughter-in-law are moving our work forward. Since Fukushima, our environment has become even more toxic. We believed that we would need plants to help us clean the air, so we have been working on hybrids that neutralize the toxic effects of the environment around us. Your son and daughter-in-law have been creating new hybrid plants and analyzing them to further refine our search for the best plants to restore the health of the atmosphere. This way, we introduce nothing foreign into the seed lines but learn much about what is most favorable. Now these plants are planted throughout our town and in many of our homes. People are getting healthier and the atmosphere is improving. It is a small but exciting beginning."

"Yes, indeed," I said. "That is wonderful news." The next thing he said was even more exciting.

Mr. Yamakazi continued with his explanation. "Your son and daughter-in-law helped us to reach a deeper understanding of the mission of my company."

I asked, "What does purposefulness have to do with genetics?"

"We conducted experiments and soon proved that what they were saying was true."

"What is that?" I asked.

"They proved that the protective qualities of these plants were altered by a purposeful beginning, or what you would call intention. When their experiments were not reproducible by others in our company, I dismissed them as anomalies, but it made no sense to me that their plants outperformed those of others in the lab."

He picked up an empty tea cup. "I understand that pottery is your hobby. I am not a maker of pots or fine china like this teacup, but I have learned much about the composition of ceramic materials like the teacup from which you are drinking your tea. This cup is fired at a much higher temperature than the fires you can build back home. This changes the properties of the teacup."

"I know that the very high temperatures used to make objects like this teacup give them their own distinctive properties. Even colors disappear. Then I thought differently about those plant experiments. I thought about the transformation that takes place in the ceramics during the firing process. I thought that perhaps your son and daughter-in-law were firing the seeds in their experiments through the power of their intentions.

"I wanted to learn more about them, so I asked Degen and Juanita about their personal histories. I learned much about the time that they have been together and, most interestingly, about the circumstances of their meeting. I knew that I needed to meet Degen's parents before I completed carrying out the rest of my plan."

"What do you mean?" I asked.

"They brought a gift to my company at exactly the right time. I believe that they have been sent here to educate me. I wanted to meet the man that brought them together."

"They are their own people, Mr. Yamakazi. At most, I am a catalyst."

"Yes, I know; that is precisely what they are to this company—catalysts. At this stage in our company's development, they are the most important catalysts I could have imagined possible. I have invested huge sums of money in order to understand how to effect meaningful changes in plants to try to heal the air in my country, and because of these plants the oxygen levels have increased and the concentration of pollutants has decreased. Good things have taken place through our efforts, but I have come to believe that I was looking in the wrong place in my quest to find more powerful answers because I did not know what to look for. I am certain you know what I mean."

"Yes, I do know what you mean."

He continued. "Degen and Juanita told me that they began each day with meditation to align themselves with their purpose, with love, and with peace. This purpose included the important technical work that caught the attention of my company. I wondered what technical work had to do with meditation. As a scientist, I did not know what to do, but it has led to the refining of my own intentions. I am now firing my own intentions at a much higher temperature than before."

He laughed and said, "I realized that even these marvelous plants would do more if we aligned our purpose with the deeper purpose of each seed, a purpose that is invisible to all our highly specialized testing methods."

He paused before he went on. "But how does one measure the intention of a seed? If we cooperate with the intent in each tiny seed, with each bit of potential, imagine what might happen!

"I felt both changed by these new experiments and more than grateful. I wanted to meet both of you because I want your son and daughter-in-law to lead this company forward with this intention—I will retire soon. They are connected with a fire that can transform and make things new…Now I sound less like a scientist and more like a monk!"

He laughed again and continued telling Pen and me about his plans.

"I have started them on a new project to begin investigating the need for such an intention-driven technology in China, a place where industrialization is destroying the air. We have wondered if our hybrid plants can also improve its atmosphere. We conducted initial talks with Chinese scientists and learned something that added a new piece to the puzzle."

"What is that?" I asked.

"There is an interesting anomaly in the deteriorating air quality that we discovered in central China, where the atmosphere is unusually pure despite the pollution, which I'm afraid I cannot discuss at length at this time. I sent Degen and Juanita there with a team of our scientists to investigate the plants that are found there."

I was thinking about Mr. Yamakazi's words. What kind of catalyst was I?

That night I had a dream:

*As I walk along a river, in the distance I see what I think is a campfire. As I get closer, I realize that it is a fire made to harden pots. A small, thin man is kneeling before the fire. As I watch, others appear and sit around the fire. Before each person sits down, they take something from their pockets and give it to him. The man adds these to the fire, which makes it brighter, hotter, and more intense.*

*When I approach, he tells me it is my turn to add something to the fire. I don't know what he means. Before I can stop him, he removes my glasses. I am afraid of not being able to see. He adds them to the fire, and the fire becomes so intense that I need to move further away or be burned by it, but my feet will not move. I stare into the fire and see the outline of the pot.*

*It is moving on its own within the fire, spinning like a top. Within the fire, a hand appears. One of the fingers touches the surface of the pot, inscribing something on the pot. Then the hand disappears and the pot stops spinning. The man reaches into the fire, but his hands and fingers are not scarred or burned by the heat.*

*He hands me the pot, which does not burn my hands. Instead, I feel an intense heat in my chest. The pot is inscribed with the letters EBKILFGN. I look around and notice that my vision is perfect even though my glasses were consumed in the fire. The other people who sat by the fire are gone.*

I woke up.

We returned from our visit to Japan, and a few months later we were invited to the region of China in which Degen and Juanita had set up their laboratory. Their discoveries were so intriguing that they invited us to come.

"It's right up your alley, Dad," Degen said. He told us that there was a small region in China that showed superior air quality. They had yet to discover any unusual plants, wind conditions, water sources, or anything else that would explain this purity.

Degen explained, "None of the plants here appear to be similar to the ones in Japan that are improving air quality. Our research team is unable to figure out what makes this small area stand out, and none of the test findings are more than suggestive about the cause."

Pen told Degen and Juanita that we would love to come and visit, so it would appear that we would soon be off on another adventure, this time to China. I thought to myself that we might be just the right catalysts.

## CHAPTER 11

# *CHINA*

A couple of nights before we left for China, I had another dream.

*I stand at the edge of the Yangtze River. I want to cross, but it is too wide and too deep and the current is too swift. I walk along the banks of the river looking for a safe place to cross. Soon I reach a man with a small boat, and the man says that he will take me across the river. It is the professor. He takes me to the other side, and during our passage, I see that the water is teeming with fish of different sizes and shapes. Flying fish leap out of the water, some even leaping across the bow. The professor, my captain, does not seem to notice. When we reach the shore, he points in the direction of a rice paddy and says, "You are nearly there."*

*I walk toward the paddy until I reach the edge of it. Several hundred yards away, a woman wearing a green dress stands in the middle of the paddy. There is a beam of light projecting from the top of her head into the sky. When I get closer, I realize that she is not standing in the paddy. She is in fact floating above it, as if the beam of light is a piece of silk that suspends her just above the water. I stare at her and study the string of light that holds her above the paddy.*

*She notices me and smiles. When I smile back, both she and the paddy disappear. I find myself in a circular room with no doors or windows that has so many large pots against the walls that they, too form a circle. I counted twelve pots in all. I walk around the room, wondering what is inside them.*

*There is a circular opening at the top of the room that a string is being lowered through. A green caterpillar crawls down the string. I move closer to it; it inches onto my finger before it instantaneously turns into a butterfly. It flies around the room, briefly hovering over each of the pots before landing in the center of the room. The butterfly turns into the woman who hovered above the paddy.*

*She walks over to the first pot, kneels down, and puts her hands on each side of the pot. The green color of her dress becomes so brilliant that I can't look directly at it, so bright it's like trying to look directly at the sun. When she stands up, her dress returns to its original color. The same thing happens with each of the pots she touches. After she touches the twelfth pot, she invites me to come near her.*

*She takes my hand and puts it into the last pot. I withdraw my hand, which is now filled with rice seeds. I know that I am supposed to throw them into the air, but I hesitate. She nods gently and I throw them into the air. Instead of falling to the ground, they organize quickly into a flock of seeds that circles around the walls of the room above the pots. The woman disappears and the butterfly flits about the center of the room.*

*Now the motion of the seeds changes as they organize themselves into patterns resembling butterflies and hover over each pot. Then the butterfly flies out of the opening in the top of the room and the seeds that had organized themselves into butterflies follow out of the opening one by one.*

I woke up after this and, like with so many other dreams, I expected that this dream's meaning would be revealed at a later time.

Before long we were in China and listening to Juanita and Degen tell us about their work. Degen explained that they had not yet found a plant similar to their hybrids in Japan and that there was one town in this particular region that captured their attention. Juanita described the labor intensive, high-tech analysis of so much data.

Pen and I were not scientists, so Degen and Juanita tried to translate the technical work into something we could understand. They shared the basic concept of photosynthesis to help us appreciate what they were seeking. I think we understood the version they gave us, but it reminded me of a high school science class for dummies.

It seemed to me that much of their work was based on the belief that if they could break everything down into individual parts, and then break each one of those parts into more parts and so on, eventually there would be no more parts to discover and all of the answers would be self-evident. I did not have the makings of a scientific brain—that was evident. Maybe this was due to a lack of intelligence, maybe a lack of interest. I would get lost in some of the little parts because of the disappearance of the big picture.

I knew that Degen and Juanita were the scientists, not me, but I also thought that my out-of-the-box experiences were a personal confirmation that the impressive science of Degen's company was just another box. It was a fancy, impressive, and expensive box, but it was still only a box. Degen and Juanita knew this, too, at some level. I was sure of it. I thought that Mr. Yamakazi knew this, too. The company's tools were made for exploring the contents of a box, and I wondered what resources would be needed to go beyond it.

Thanks to Degen and Juanita, we were given a simplified reeducation of photosynthesis: Plants use light and carbon dioxide to grow and produce oxygen.

Degen took a few more concepts out of the photosynthesis box and said, "The part of this that doesn't make any sense is the part that has to do with light-dependent reactions. We didn't find anything unusual with the other parts—the light-independent reactions. I know you won't remember all the parts within these categories: The enzymes, the biophysical structures or biochemical reactions that describe the relationships between these little parts...Anyway, we also didn't find anything anomalous about the water, the soil, or the climate."

He continued. "Plants normally convert sunlight into chemical energy with an efficiency of only a few percent, but there are some plants in this region that can convert light more efficiently into energy than a solar panel.

"The light-dependent reactions are possible because of remarkable structures in plants that are able to harvest the light."

Degen went on to describe even more tiny parts, including chlorophyll and other pigments that are part of light-harvesting structures. It was interesting, but I did get lost in some of the details because there were so many parts in the photosynthesis box. Even so, I held on to the big picture.

Juanita explained how they used instruments to measure which wavelengths of light were accepted by the pigments of the photosystem and how efficiently these wavelengths produced energy. She said that some of the light was reemitted as fluorescence and that other energy was lost as heat. Juanita also reminded us that the familiar green color of the plants was the reflection of what light the plants didn't use, although there were some organisms that were able to use different wavelengths and appeared in different colors.

Degen added that analysis of the area led them to consider rice as a key plant. One particular field of rice was being closely studied and compared with rice paddies nearby. While the air quality was different above the fields, the testing did not find any differences between the photosystems. The absorption spectra were identical.

I thought about my dream and the blinding brilliance of her dress when the woman touched the seed pot.

"Have you checked the entire spectrum?" I asked.

Degen replied, "We check all known frequency ranges for any species that performs photosynthesis."

I said, "I think you should look in a different place, at much higher frequencies that are beyond the visible spectrum of light."

Degen said, "That doesn't make any sense, Dad."

"I'm sure it doesn't, but humor me. Just try it."

It's mind boggling to think about what might be found outside of our boxes. Far beyond what was ever considered to be relevant to photosynthesis, Degen and Juanita discovered a new band of absorption with a greater intensity than had ever been measured in the visible spectrum from that anomalous paddy. The band was not found in the rice from any of the other paddies. Much effort went into the search for the new pigment, but nothing was found to explain the high energy absorption.

Pen suggested that we visit the town and surrounding area, and I thought that was an excellent idea.

The next day we walked through the town and I felt pulled in a particular direction, so we headed to the edge of town. We could see the banks of the Yangtze River, and there was a group of people farming in the area. I wondered if the meaning of my dream might be found over there.

Only a few days later, the answer to the question of the anomalous rice paddy stood before my family and me.

"It's her," I said to Pen as I pointed her out. "It's the woman who was in my dream."

She was wrapping the small plants into bundles to be transplanted into the paddy.

"She is the reason for the band that cannot be explained," I insisted. "She is the light-harvesting complex. She is the one who activates and awakens a new photosystem in the rice. It is a virtual pigment that we can't see or measure, but it is there."

We watched her from a distance as butterflies danced around her while she worked. Sometimes they landed on her head for a moment before moving to a spot near her. I imagined her talking to the pots that held the seeds before they were planted. At just that moment, she looked up and smiled.

"Let's go and meet her," I said.

We met our answer, and she was quite radiant. She and I recognized each other, if that was even possible. From where, I could not say, but we recognized each other.

I turned to Degen and said, "Here is your answer."

Additional analysis confirmed that the air quality in the paddy began to improve at the time of her birth. The area of clean air was slowly expanding despite the building of a new power plant no more than ten miles upwind of the paddy.

Is that really possible? Her name was Liu-Wo, and she cultivated plants with her family members, just as they had for generations. We found an interpreter and heard the story of her birth and of her early years. She was known by all as someone who loved the Earth, especially the plants. She talked to them. She sang to them. She blessed them.

Apparently there was something much more important that should have been considered than another plant to study for its traits and properties. Juanita said, "Our focus has been too narrow to look beyond the plants. It didn't occur to us to think about who did the planting and how it was done, but now we have found the answer: Liu-Wo. The plants flourish because she is the key ingredient."

Juanita was right. I wondered what would happen if this girl were in Tibet or in Shanghai. We needed to clean the atmosphere of so much unnecessary chatter, noise, toxicity, and hatred. The fact that this change in the air quality might come through the one doing the planting and not the plant itself or its seeds was the message. Our son and daughter-in-law would bring these findings back to Japan and create more momentum and excitement for their work and for the Japanese CEO, Mr. Yamakazi.

I tried to imagine what it would be like if there were thousands like Liu-Wo. Eventually, all of these pockets of cleanliness and sanity would merge into one, and the toxicity would simply have no place to go. Now that's what I call a real catalyst.

# CHAPTER 12

## *INDIA*

Pen was working on a new painting when the call came. Another set of findings led Degen and Juanita to consider a new project in eastern India, so they'd gone there. Their research indicated more anomalies that were similar to the one discovered in China. They wanted us to come visit them in India.

After we ended our conversation with them, Pen said, "It is another sign, darling. I guess we are off on another adventure."

The next morning Pen invited me into her studio. I watched her paint a picture of eastern India inside a rainbow-colored circle.

She looked at me and said, "I have an idea about how we can help them. I thought we could tell them where to meet us."

Pen continued. "Haven't we learned by now that the information we need is always available if we ask for it? Let us each do our part to describe the path by drawing two lines. The intersection of the lines will be a location of light, coherency, and evolved consciousness. I will draw the first line; you can draw the second one."

Pen shifted her focus to a painting of an orchid that she'd recently completed. While she gazed at the orchid, she put her right hand on top of the circle she just finished painting. She traced her fingers slowly around the still-wet paint of the rainbow circle and then stopped. She marked the spot with a small dot. She continued to trace the circle with her fingers, stopping at a second point and marking it. Pen took her fingers off the circle and picked up a very fine brush, drawing a straight line between the two points.

"Now it's your turn," she said.

Pen gave me her brush. Beginning at the twelve o'clock position of the circle, I traced the rainbow with my index finger. My eyes were open, but my mind took me beyond the simple image of eastern India inside the circle.

Although I stood motionless before the canvas, I imagined that I was walking in an unfamiliar place. Soon I reached the edge of a river. When I reached the edge, my index finger stopped moving around the circle. I used Pen's brush and marked the first point. My index finger started to move around the circle again as I mentally waded slowly into the river. A fish moved toward me. It settled next to my leg as if my leg was a post that supported a dock under which the fish took refuge. When the fish stopped moving, I marked the second spot on the circle and mentally waded back to the dry land. I connected the two spots by drawing a straight line between them.

We found the point of intersection on the map of east India, and Pen took a photo of the map with the intersecting lines. We sent it to Degen and Juanita so they could meet us there.

Pen laughed and said, "I think we just made a treasure map."

That night I had a dream.

*I walk along a narrow trail that winds along the slope of a steep, rocky mountain. There are mountains all around me. I look below the trail and see a river thousands of feet below where I am standing. It is foggy and not easy to see the small path ahead of me, but I keep going. The path becomes rockier and more difficult to find as I climb higher and higher. I look down again, but now I am too high to see the river. The fog is also thicker, so dense that I can barely see the ground ahead of me. I am afraid to move forward for fear of stumbling or getting lost. I decide to wait for the fog to clear so that I can take another step.*

*From behind me, I hear a sound. I listen as the sound grows louder and know that it is footsteps. There is a second sound, too, but I don't know what it is. The footsteps are getting close to me. I look back and see the silhouettes of a man and an animal heading toward me. The second silhouette is a mountain goat.*

*The man says, "There you are. Follow me."*

*I follow him and the mountain goat up the mountain for a while. We come to what looks like a dead end. It is an enormous wall of granite. He touches his walking stick to the granite and says, "This is the way."*

*When his stick touches the stone, there is a thunderous sound. I am afraid an avalanche that will throw us down the mountain has started. I open my eyes to see that the granite wall has split into three enormous boulders. The third boulder lies across the other two like the top of a table. It reminds me of the rock formation in Spain at the entrance to the* balnearios.

*"Come, Dolmen," the man says.*

*I follow him and the goat through the opening, and we ascend an elaborate circular stairway. I count the steps as we move higher. On the twelfth step, I emerge from the passageway onto the top of the mountain. The fog is gone and it is brilliantly sunny. I look above me to see only light. In the distance I see the peaks of many mountains poking up through the clouds. I look below me and realize that it was not fog that made it difficult to see. I had been in the clouds, and now we are far above them. I feel safe. I want to stay here to look around. It seems that from this vantage point, there is no limit to what I can see no matter what direction I look.*

*From behind me, I feel my guide move toward me. He places his hands on my shoulders while I continue to bathe in the beauty of what is before me. He says to me, "You see, there is only the Light. In every direction, there is only the Light. Behind every appearance, there is only the Light."*

*He removes his hands from my shoulders. I turn around to thank him, but when I turn around, both the man and the goat are gone, vanished. Only his walking stick remains, lying on the ground at my feet. I pick up the walking stick.*

I awoke from the dream feeling immensely peaceful and alive. My intuition told me that the man who guided me to the top of the mountain was Professor Ebkilfgn. I tried to imagine that I was holding his walking stick, and the more I tried to feel it, the more the experience felt like the time I held the bowl in his classroom.

From the top of the mountain in that dream, I realized that the beautiful, benevolent light was eternal and always present. It was a matter of limited perception to not know this. The clouds blocking this light moved with the changing weather patterns of our lives, but beyond them lay the truth. No matter where I lived or what happened or what I thought I knew, it was cloudy, but behind every cloud there was eternal light. With my eyes open, it was just as easy to say the opposite—no matter where you are, contrary to all appearances, there is only light.

Mr. Yamakazi's company made all of the arrangements for our trip to India. We stayed in the town closest to the intersection on the map we made for Degen and Juanita.

It came as no surprise to us that the intersection on our treasure map matched one of the zones of exceptionally clean air. Pen and I believed that the company could not have chosen a better location using its sophisticated tools than we had with Pen's brush and canvas back home. Our best tool was the power of intention given by the Great Unseen.

The town was less than five miles from the area indicated on our map. We were in the vicinity of this pocket of clean air—we could feel it. I wondered if its source might be something besides a close relative of the plant Degen and Juanita hoped to find. I thought about meeting Liu-Wo and what we learned in China. Maybe this was another case in which we were looking in the right place, but for the wrong object. Maybe the source was not an object. It was exciting to be with Degen and Juanita and to be involved in the quest for the answer.

The answer did not come quickly or easily. We were not discouraged, though we admitted to feeling some impatience. Degen and Juanita didn't find any of the plants that would confirm of their growing theory about the source of the improved atmosphere, and there was another problem that we did not expect: The location of the clean air moved, sometimes by as much as several miles in a single day. We were puzzled.

The four of us returned to the location of the intersection on the map. We were standing at the intersection of two small trails, looking at the map and trying to decide which direction to go when we noticed a young man leading a small herd of goats approaching us.

Degen said, "We better move off the path so he can keep his herd together."

The boy waved as if he knew us and I suggested we stay to meet the boy.

As he moved closer to us, I felt an electrical sensation in my hands. I knew we were in the right place at the right time. I thought to myself that there is a lot to be said for timing. A minute sooner or later and we would not have seen him heading in our direction. I saw the staff in his hand and remembered my dream.

I was surprised that he spoke English, and he spoke it plainly enough that it was impossible to miss his optimism and enthusiasm when he greeted us.

I did not visually recognize him when I met him, but I thought of my dream and believed that both of us had visited that same destination beyond the clouds and through the mountain. We shared the same exhilaration about an endless vista above the clouds that transformed all beliefs about what lay beyond the ceiling of the clouds.

The young man said, "Yes, it is meant to be that we meet here right now, in this very moment! This is the land upon which my animals graze, and yes, we are exactly where we need to be. I bless these animals, the grasses that they eat, the soil that holds these grasses for them, and the holy ones who live within the soil. My name is Nradah, and this is my home."

The young shepherd was so happy, so friendly, so joyful! He was dressed in ordinary clothes, and he was dusty. I noticed that his hands were calloused and very dirty. How could such a poor boy be so joyful?

His enthusiasm and love for life was not limited to just human beings and his goats. I remember when Nradah said, "Live not just on the soil, or live to use the soil, but live in the soil. Yes, indeed I think this is what allows us to walk upon it. I know that the holy ones bless these grasses; it is the holy ones that hold these roots and live within them. The holy ones feed my sheep just as they feed me." I think what he meant to tell us was that he loved the earth.

Nradah bent down and picked up a handful of dirt, telling us that we were dirt too—blessed dirt.

He looked up at the sky and said, "Yes, blessed dirt. Every bit of it is blessed."

As I listened to him, it dawned on me that Nradah was the reason for the purified air. The clean air moved when and where he moved with his flock. He was a living expression of joy.

He looked at me with great love and hope as he interrupted my thoughts and confirmed that we knew one another and traveled the same path. He said, "I have met others, but they are not quite like you and me."

He laughed and said, "You and I are like family, but due to circumstances we are only meeting for the first time. There are other families too, though, and they have been there, too. I'm sure there will be others."

I said, "I hope so."

Nradah smiled and said, "It could not be otherwise."

I knew that later I could speak of such matters with Pen, Degen, and Juanita. I was even certain that Mr. Yamakazi would understand, as well. Perhaps I would even go and see him about it. I was not certain what I would do, but the thought occurred to me that the CEO of an impressive Japanese scientific corporation might one day be led up the mountain as I was. I smiled at the thought of this and at how enjoyable it would be to talk about this adventure over tea.

I wondered if Nradah would test positive for the same absorption band that escaped the notice of the experts. Perhaps the absorption band was evidence of the development of an invisible structure within his being that formed as a consequence of his attunement to the Light. Perhaps the band was incredibly intense and coherent, and perhaps it emitted pure joy because his young body could not possibly contain all of it. Could there be a better explanation for joy?

I thought that such a band might be forming in me as these structures continued to develop in my own body. Maybe many of the important people in my life whom I never could have imagined considering family were also developing similar structures that radiated love, peace, and joy throughout the world.

I dared to believe that the potential to create a structure capable of absorbing the gifts of the holy ones was within the capacity of every human being. I dared to wonder what the world would be like if this was our purposeful intent. Would there be any bad air left? Would there be any more clouds to obscure whatever was beyond the veil? The Source of existence was constantly sending us an infinite supply of light that all of us could harvest.

I wondered if Professor Ebkilfgn's mission was to awaken his family to the work of receiving and transmitting this Light. It was beyond my intellectual reach to understand it any further, but somehow I felt that Nradah understood what I was trying to say perfectly.

The young shepherd boy lived the truth of the Light. Although he carried a simple shepherd's staff, it was his intention that guided him. He knew that wherever he took his goats, there was only Light. He knew that in every blade of grass, in every drop of rain, in every bit of soil, there was only Light. While it might seem to others that our meeting was highly unlikely, I believed that it was providential. Apparently, he also believed every moment in his life could be described in the same joyful way. No matter where he traveled with his herd of goats, it seemed to me that he never lost the ability to see everything from the top of the mountain beyond the clouds. This was true regardless of the day, the place, or the weather. Of course it would be perfectly obvious to him that he was meeting us at exactly the right moment. I laughed to myself and thought that Nradah must have been in the same anthropology classroom as me so many years ago, although I knew that didn't make logical sense. I imagined that the staff he carried was cut from the same tree as the walking stick in my dream.

We could all be light harvesters. That was my thought on that day, and it is still what I think today. We will not harvest our light by taking a drug to give us all the chemical ingredients for a new photosystem or by implanting a solar panel in our forehead. Purchasing it with money earmarked to acquire a new technology would never work—indeed, it would only cheapen it. The only way for anyone to acquire the Light, regardless of their socioeconomic status, is by working on themselves, by aligning with the divine. Intent—loving intent—will birth the system in anyone. Anyone can know the Light that stands behind and beyond every appearance. Intention can birth the virtual pigment from an invisible domain where the Great Unseen resides. When enough of this Holy Light is collected, anyone can radiate love, peace, joy, and, as a byproduct, clean air.

When I told the others that the superior air quality was a manifestation of the shepherd and not a new plant, they were only mildly surprised. I was relieved by their reactions. They were disappointed when I told them that there were no new plants to study in the area, but as I told them about the young man, it opened exciting possibilities in their minds instead of disappointment, even though this was not necessarily good news for a company that set out to make money from a new discovery that could be sold to a hungry market. We talked about the idea that the untapped gifts of human beings could transform a toxic world not through new technologies, but through the daily task of attending to a higher purpose. The opportunity to attune to the holy ones, as Nradah described it, lay within the grasp of everyone. No sophisticated tools were required. If a shepherd boy could manifest these subtle structures, then surely others could do the same and were doing so, just as he'd said to me.

Juanita spoke first. "We will honor what the young man is doing here by not sharing his name. He is not a specimen for a laboratory experiment. As with Liu-Wo, he is a sign to everyone to look beyond the spectrum of what we know—of what we think we know."

Degen added, "I look forward to sharing these findings with Mr. Yamakazi. I believe he will be further intrigued and inspired by what we have learned here in India."

I thought of Mr. Yamakazi. I thought of the dream I'd had in which the man brightened the fire by collecting the prized possessions of those who gathered around the fire. He'd burned my glasses, which were presumably necessary for me to see things clearly. I imagined this man gathering technical papers containing information that came with considerable time and expense. I thought of him adding these papers to the fire, discarding still more of what was considered essential to understanding how to improve the environment. I wondered if he might consider this work my family was doing in India to be tinder for creating the possibility of an even hotter, more intense fire of understanding or an invitation to move beyond the territory of conventional science and into a new land.

Eventually we returned home and our son and daughter-in-law went back to Japan. I had so much to consider. Timing is a divine intersection; everything comes together for a reason. Is it not possible to remain indefinitely at this intersection when neither past nor future exist and there is only the present moment? That would be a moment of inexplicable joy and brilliance when you are seeing everything from the top of the mountain!

# CHAPTER 13

## *KENYA*

Our daughter and son-in-law finished their appointment in Mozambique and were reassigned to Kenya. We worried because there was an escalating civil war, and due to recent political upheavals, their organization was on the wrong side as far as the government was concerned. We were worried about David, Lana, and the kids, and there was not a ban on travel to Kenya, so we decided to go see them. Pen and I ignored any advice we received to stay home and any discouragement about visiting them. I thought about how unfamiliar and strange Mozambique had been. Could it be worse in Kenya?

At least on the outside, it seemed to be a more dangerous and uncertain situation. We felt the difference the moment we stepped off the plane. The suspiciousness and hostility of the soldiers toward foreigners was unmistakable. We avoided meeting the stares of the soldiers and calmly headed out of the airport. Just outside the door, Pen spotted a man holding a sign with our names on it. We followed the man to his dusty SUV, where he loaded Pen's suitcase and we quickly got in. A Christian logo was displayed prominently on the side of the car, and we asked him if it was a shield of protection or a target.

Our driver answered without giving a direct answer when he told us we needed to take a longer route to bypass government checkpoints. Our logo would not necessarily protect us, and it might attract unwanted attention. The label "American" would also not ensure our safety.

It was a long and dusty ride, but, nonetheless, it was beautiful. We did not stop. The driver told us we could not stop for any reason. He said that it was not safe after dark even on the best roads available to us. We wondered what we would find. Lookouts informed the village of our approach nearly an hour before our arrival because they could not afford the risk of a government surprise. We wondered and worried about the safety and wisdom of both the timing of our visit and our kids accepting this assignment.

Soon we could see David and Lana and their two children standing with a few others in the distance. Everybody was waving, and I was happy to know that they appeared to be all right. We felt elated and relieved. I looked for but could not detect signs of worry or fear in any of them.

We didn't see any other fair-skinned people or government soldiers, but I did not sense tension between our family and the villagers. We wanted to learn more, to be with our grandchildren and hear their laughter, to hold them and listen to them. We learned that their assignment, which was intended to develop safe water and electricity in this region and train locals in healthcare services, had lost its government sanctions. David told us there were some government officials who might accuse them of helping the rebels, but he said that their village was neutral.

Lana said, "But it is difficult to be neutral here. There is pressure from both sides to declare loyalties."

I said, "This cannot be safe for you or your children."

Lana replied, "Since we've been here, I've learned much from one of the elders. Her name is Faith Kdajaja. She said she knows you."

I asked, "She knows me?" I laughed and said, "Why, of course she knows me. I would be happy to meet her. I want to get a better idea of what is going on here—"

Lana interrupted. "Dad, she already knows you. She just wants to meet you face to face."

"And how is that possible?" I inquired.

"Faith told me that she could tell by how I walk on the earth that the man who is my father is her kin, too—part of her family."

I did not expect these words from Lana, but inside, I knew that she was right.

The next morning I met Faith Kdajaja in the flesh. She was a thick, stocky woman with a commanding, powerful presence. She was strong and gentle at the same time. I learned much that day. She told me that a good way to begin was to share a pipe, so we did. While we smoked the pipe, she spoke of our bond.

"The bones told me that I would see you before I go to be with my ancestors. It is good to be with you on this side of the river."

Her laugh was familiar, reminiscent of someone from long ago—an aunt, perhaps—although I could not exactly place it or label it. With her finger, she drew a circle on the ground, and then another and then another.

Faith said, "The government lives in this circle, the rebels in this one, the villagers in this one, and still there are many more circles."

She drew more and more circles for more and more villages. Then she said, "The villagers think that this is their circle, so they must swear loyalty to those in their circle. They are told to be afraid and protect themselves from anybody who does not live in their circle. The rebels and the government want us to believe in and live in their circles. I've thought about this many times, especially when our circles have been broken by hatred and violence. Fear makes these circles smaller and more brittle."

She drew a very tiny circle, laughed, and said, "Now who could live in such a small circle, in such a tiny place?"

She continued with the following story: "A few months ago, my granddaughter was away from our village, out in the country and way outside of our circle. Government soldiers stopped her, beat and raped her, and left her for dead. She was badly injured but alive. She managed to find her way home back to this circle. Your daughter helped her recover from her injuries. Lana saved her life. She was still broken on the inside, but she was not dead. My granddaughter healed from her physical injuries but is still wounded by what the soldiers did to her. No doctor or nurse can fix that. I wondered what more I could do to help her. I did not know what to do, what anyone could do."

Faith stared at the ground. She said, "I thought about the foolishness of all these circles and how these circles harmed my granddaughter. I remembered that the former rebel leaders who were no longer in power had done so many of the same things. I wondered who started it. Did it matter to me? I decided that it didn't matter. There were just so many circles, and one was no different than another. My granddaughter belonged to one. The soldiers belonged to another. Are there not granddaughters in every circle? Are there not old women in every circle? Are there not young, angry men in every circle?

"I wondered how long this would go on. How many more angry young men would agree to continue this hatred and violence?"

Faith stood up and drew a larger circle around all of the smaller circles. She said, "This larger circle is me, Dolmen. All of these little circles are inside of me. My boundaries have expanded each time that I try to have compassion for all, no matter what circle they say is their own. I decided that they are not so much guilty as foolish and clueless. No circle is somehow different or better than any other. I try not to take any sides but see every person who is hurting as someone I can help. I don't care about their circle."

As I listened to her, I thought her name suited her well.

Faith continued. "This has taken courage and made me strong. Let me tell you a story: One day, a government soldier broke his leg. He was found not far from our village by one of our villagers. The man who found him was not sure if he should help him, so he ran back to the village and asked me what to do. I told him to bring the soldier here so I could set his leg. Some of the people in our village were afraid. They worried that if the rebels found out about it, they would think we were harboring their enemy and attack our village. I told them the villager must bring the soldier to me because he needed our help. They agreed with reluctance, resentment, anger, and fear.

"I reset the young man's leg and gave him medicine and food. While ministering to him, I inquired about his family and learned that his brothers and parents had been killed and his sister had been sold into the sex trade. I wept with him for what had happened to his family.

"He was very grateful for being found, brought to the village, and given the care he needed.

"The soldier said, 'I can never repay you for what you have done. You saved my life. When I return home, I will send you a gift from the government.'

"I said, 'That is very kind of you. Thank you for your generosity, but my prayer is that when you return home, you will help your friends to understand that these rebels who are your enemies are as grieved by such tragedies as you have shared with me. We have wept together over so many great and unnecessary losses in your life.'

"The soldier protested. 'That is not possible. Why did you help me?'

"I said to him, 'Because that is what I do.'

"Then I told him what happened to my granddaughter. After I finished the story, I introduced him to her. The young man fell to his knees because he recognized her. He was among the group of soldiers who had violated her. My granddaughter also recognized him as one of her tormentors.

"Then my granddaughter said the most remarkable thing. She said, 'I forgive you.'

"The soldier sobbed. I think it was almost too much for him to bear that the woman they'd left for dead was alive and telling him that she forgave him. Maybe the soldier realized that he could have easily been eaten by a lion if not for the compassion of our village. In that moment of forgiveness, I believe that my granddaughter found what was missing to heal her, and it was the same for the soldier. My granddaughter's smile has returned. The soldier left with more than a healed leg. The circles became greater.

"Soon after that, we heard that our village was no longer suspected by the government of harboring rebels. Whether we're dealing with rebel or government, it really doesn't matter to me—change the costumes, but it is all the same...Still all circles. In every circle, everyone has family, everyone has children, everyone bleeds, and everyone dies. We may look or act differently on the outside, but on the inside we are all the same.

"One day I hope the soldier will share this larger circle with me. Beyond right and wrong, there is only one great circle. This Earth is one great circle in a sea of still greater circles. Is this not true?"

Faith continued. "I cannot guarantee the safety of your family, especially outside of this village, although things have become much safer since these events. I know that their work here expands the greater circle and that it doesn't matter which side you're on and in whose circle you reside."

She laughed. "Earlier in my life, I changed sides many times—sometimes without even knowing it! Others told me that I had done so through something I did or didn't do, but how can someone else tell you what side you're on? As I got older, I wanted no part in this. I only wanted the sides to disappear."

With that, she used her hand to sweep away all of the circles she had drawn on the ground.

We stayed in Kenya for a few more weeks, long enough to see progress in the project and a tentative peace agreement. I thought that the true broker of this agreement was Faith Kdajaja. Lana told us that the new government leader was the soldier whose broken leg she'd fixed. He had become a man of peace. At least one of the circles was now sufficiently large enough for the people on each side of this conflict to discuss what they held in common.

We felt better about David, Lana, and the grandkids being there for a few more years.

On the long plane ride back home, I fell asleep and had the following dream:

*I am sitting at my potter's wheel, but it is in the middle of a vast and brightly lit space that feels like a white room without walls, corners, or edges. In every direction, I see nothing. I am sitting on a chair, but it is not the chair from my shed. As I stare out into the distance, eventually I can make out the outline of mountains. I think that my potter's wheel and I are on top of a flat expanse of stone that has no beginning or end. The only sound I hear is the turning of my wheel. I listen to its sound and it reminds me of the deep hum of the* balnearios.

*I look at my hands as they mold the clay into the shape of a small pot. I see my hands change into those of a child and the pot grows larger. My hands change again into those of a young woman. The pot grows larger still, and I notice that its color is changing, too. My hands continue to change, every age and race participating in the throwing of this pot. It grows larger and larger. The pot is so immense and the wheel has grown so large that I can't see across the pot to the other side. Its walls have become thick like a fortress. It is the size of a stadium. The pot continues to grow, and my hands continue to change.*

*The wheel stops and I realize the pot is so large that I can no longer comprehend its size. I stand up to look into the pot and see that it is filled with water, like a vast swimming pool or even an ocean. There are people swimming and relaxing in the huge pool inside the pot. The people are of all ages and nationalities. Everyone is happy and the sounds of laughter ring out. I decide to join them and climb over the edge of the pot to get into the water.*

When I wake up, I feel happy and cheerful. I hear the captain say that we are almost ready to land and that we are on time.

# CHAPTER 14

## *BULGARIA*

It was good to be home again. Our routines were peaceful and purposeful. I think Pen and I discovered through all of our travels a new sense of coherency; everything had found a way of fitting together, not just in a physical sense but spiritually, too. We had been blessed beyond any reasonable expectation with the expansion of our family through a non-biological mechanism that was activated with intention and assured through grace. The years passed quickly and with ease.

Degen and Juanita remained in Japan, updating us from time to time about their work. Mr. Yamakazi turned over the leadership of his company to them as he had told us he one day would.

Lana and David finished their second mission in Africa and moved to a home within a day's drive of our home. We enjoyed being with them and watching Ida and Doren grow up. Time passed by quickly in increments of one month and then one year and then another.

I thought of many things and have endeavored to share them with you in this book, dear reader. It was during these quiet years at home that I decided to write about the experiences of my life. I wondered if everything had been written that needed to be said. More than twenty years had passed since our trip to Kenya. I wondered if I would ever take another trip or make any new discoveries. One night I dreamed of the coffee shop where the man had given me the card for the EBK Travel Agency. I woke up the next morning and, to amuse myself, decided I would go back there to see if it was still there.

I went back to the coffee house where the man had given me the card that sent me on a journey I would've scarcely believed. It had been so many years since I had been here, but it all looked much the same. It held the same table and chairs, the same paintings—even the cups and the silverware looked the same. Then, as I should have suspected, there was a tap on my shoulder. I was lost in my thoughts, so I hadn't seen him approach me, but this time I was not surprised.

"One last trip," he said as he placed the card next to my cup.

"The last one?" I asked.

"Yes, I believe so." He smiled. "It is the last one you signed up for—at least this time around. It has been a pleasure to cross paths with you once more."

I knew that the card would be similar to the first. I looked up, but the man was already gone. I wondered if I would ever see him again, but my intuition said that this would be the last time I would visit the coffee shop.

I thought of the dream in which the man and his goat led me up to the top of the mountain. Instead of quickly returning home, I sat at the coffee shop for quite a long time and stared at the familiar lettering and message on the card. I thought about the first time I received the same card and about Degen's worry and frustration that his dad was serious about the EBK Travel Agency and the man who gave the card to him. I thought about what happened to me on that trip, about Medir, about the *balnearios*, about Pedro and Juanita. Now Juanita and my son were together in Japan. How strange and wondrous life can be!

I thought about Nradah, the Indian shepherd who lived so completely in the present, not stuck in the fantasies of the past or the future. I had found a way to be more present in my life. Living in the present was a habitable state devoid of time or space. It was a place beyond the veil of the clouds, on top of the mountain, the passageway opened by the power of intent. Accepting the second card from the man was a final invitation that would bring an even deeper knowledge, a deeper fulfillment, and a greater coherency with the divine.

I was ready to go home and show the card to Pen. When I showed it to her, she smiled and hugged me. No explanation was necessary about what happened at the coffee shop.

Pen asked, "It is the last trip, isn't it, Dolmen?"

I held back my tears and nodded.

The next day I called the number, which I had not used for decades, and listened to the same computerized voice. This time, without hesitation I responded with the requested information. A few days later I received the itinerary. My trip was not a return trip to Spain. I was going to Bulgaria this time. I would arrive there on the day I turned seventy. By now, there was little space in me to fill with worry or doubt. There seemed little to me about life that could be described by the word "coincidence." I thanked the Great Unseen for one last journey. I knew that even with all I had learned, there was an incompleteness; something was missing, although I wasn't sure what it was.

I Skyped with Degen and Juanita the night before I left. We shared stories about our old days of adventure. Lana, David, Ida, and Doren came over in the morning for breakfast and wished me a blessed trip. Pen took me to the airport. She was serene and radiant, and I remembered how differently I handled her trip to Tibet and the three-month extension. It was time to go.

When I kissed Pen goodbye and departed for Bulgaria, I knew she would await my final return. I took the stone she gave me in Tibet out of my pocket and held it in my palm. I put her hand on top of mine, the stone sandwiched in between them. I wanted to remind her of what she had once told me, that no matter how many miles separated us physically, she was still with me and I was with her.

I said, "I will be back soon."

Pen replied, "Yes, you will be back when it is the right moment to return, and I will be here." She put her hand over my heart and said, "I will see you in here every day while you are in Bulgaria. I will be with you. I love you."

"I love you, too, Penelope."

As I sat in the plane, I wondered if I would ever see my dear Penelope in the flesh again. Maybe at this fraction of time in my human life span, the chariots were calling me home. If that was true, it still wouldn't change the truth of what Pen said to me. I was not really leaving her. I thought about her during the long flight, appreciating the woman she became through her dedication to her work—not just her love for painting, but also the canvas of her life, which she fashioned through each stroke of what she believed and intended. Pen helped me to do the same through my pottery.

I finally landed in Bulgaria. A young man stood waiting for me outside the terminal holding an EBK Travel Agency sign. I did not recognize him, but he reminded me of Pedro. Soon we were traveling together through the mountainous and remote territory of southwestern Bulgaria. The driver told me that our destination was a small town along the road that linked the West to the East, a passageway that was used for centuries. He told me that the town used to be situated along the road that Roman soldiers used to travel to distant lands. There were still ancient ruins near the town, especially along the river where the soldiers would rest and water their horses.

The road became more rugged as we travelled further and further into the mountain range, but I enjoyed seeing the huge valleys, massive pine forests, and rock formations as we passed them. I saw in the distance a small town that was bisected by a river. A stone bridge allowed passage over this river. There were only a few houses in the town, but it had a mosque and a cathedral. The driver pointed to a house next to the river a couple of miles out of town. This was the home of the travel agency.

The home was similar to the others that we passed. It was built of wood, stones, and mortar.

An older man sat in a chair on a small porch in front of the house. When we arrived, he got up and walked over to the car. He was a large man with enormous hands and forearms. He reminded me of my grandfather, who had spent his life working on a farm. I got out of the car, ready to begin another adventure/vacation.

"Good afternoon, Dolmen Wilcox, and welcome. I am Evgeni Dimitrov. I've been waiting for your arrival for some time."

His words reminded me of Medir's words in Spain—she, too, had been waiting for me to come for a much longer time than I had been planning the trip.

I said, "I am very honored to meet you." I shook his hand and knew that I was meeting another member of my family.

We shared stories and a glass of *rakia*. Evgeni was a sculptor. He grew up in the traditions of the Eastern Orthodox Church. His family moved to Bulgaria from Macedonia when he was a boy. They'd lived about two hundred miles south of his present home. He was not an educated man in the academic sense of the word, but he was a master craftsman who understood how to work with soil and rock. I suspected that he kept much of what he knew to himself. I also learned that he made excellent wine that he shared with the rest of the town.

Evgeni struck me as a man who found balance in life between work and play. A piece of sculpture and a great bottle of wine both required time and patience, not a due date. He was content to live far from the urban world and loved his simple life of creating art. He cherished the company of his wife and friends. He enjoyed the visits from outsiders who wanted to learn about his sculptures, and he ran the EBK Travel Agency on the side.

I told him about my trip to Spain and the *balnearios* and that this was the second time I'd received an invitation from the travel agency.

Evgeni said, "Yes, the *balnearios* changes everyone. If we are reborn, there is no going back, no matter where it takes you. Now it has brought you here."

He continued. "Much of what has happened to you has not only transformed *your* life, but the lives of others, too, including your family. It has also introduced you to others who are now your family."

I nodded in agreement. Evgeni did not seem surprised by anything I told him. I shared the stories of all of my travels with him. When I told him about Pen, the kids, and grandchildren, I felt like I was catching up with an old friend. It reminded me of sitting in Pablo and Calde's home back in Argentina, and I told him so. He just smiled and listened.

Over the next few days I did the best I could to explain to Evgeni what I thought I'd learned from these experiences. I told him that leaving the familiar life that I once thought would bring me happiness was the best and, probably, most irrational decision I had ever made. He listened with compassion and understanding and again, he did not seem surprised by anything I said. I wondered when he would tell me where I was headed on this trip. Would it be like going to the *balnearios*? On my third day at his home, I decided it was time to ask him about our plans.

I asked, "Will I be traveling far from the agency as I did in Spain? Where will I be going from here?"

Evgeni replied, "In a couple of days, you will make the trip. Best to rest for a while and enjoy what is here."

I asked, "Is it far from here, Evgeni?"

He laughed and said, "No, it is not too far." He pointed to a bend in the river and said, "About four hundred meters as the crow flies."

He added, "It is time for rest. We can resume our conversation in the morning."

The next morning Evgeni invited me to the sculpture garden behind his house. We walked along a path that took us past his vineyard. The sculpture garden contained a central fountain located in the center of a small pond that was surrounded by a stone walk. When I got to the pond, I noticed there were fish in it. There were also twelve stone paths that connected the circular walk around the pond like the spokes of a wheel. The paths were lined with plants. At the end of each spoke there was a sculpture made of marble surrounded by a small garden. We walked each path so I could study the sculptures. Each sculpture was of a person coming out of the block of stone. The figures were men and women, young and old, different races emerging from the marble. When I got to the last one, a block of marble sat untouched.

"What about this one?" I asked.

Evegeni said, "I still have some work to do. It is the last one, and the garden will be complete."

We walked back to the center of the garden. I looked closely at the row of stones closest to the pond and noticed that they were inscribed with the letters EBKILGN.

Before I could ask him about the letters, Evgeni told me about his work.

He said, "Every sculpture begins in the same way, Dolmen. Look over there at those mountains. Beyond them is the quarry these blocks of marble were cut from. They were placed in the locations in my garden, where they have stood for many years. Each has assumed its form as my hammer and chisel slowly removed some of the stone.

"But what is the stone? From what is the stone made? It is so hard on the outside, yes, but what about the inside? And you and I—of what are we made?"

We walked back to the first sculpture in the garden. It showed a girl looking up at the sky. Her hands were extended into the air and she was laughing.

"This was my first sculpture for the garden. The Great Unseen showed me in a dream what it would look like, and she appears here as she did to me on that night. Each sculpture is birthed from this invisible place. Inside each of these stones is its true origin. The stone exists as a consciousness beyond time and space that is filled with its own intent before I ever pick up my tools."

He pointed to the last stone, which was not yet altered by his work. He continued, "It is already there in that stone, too. You just can't see it. The intention that is buried within the stone will manifest its own information and ideas about what it is. This information creates its own energy and activities. This energy creates its own forms that appear to give it the structure and form you see."

I replied, "Like my pots—created from the empty space within."

"Yes."

"Like Pen's paintings—her heart manifesting what is already there through the brush."

"Yes."

"Like all of the others that I have met who are manifesting the power of the Great Unseen through their devotion and intention to what cannot be seen."

"Yes."

"And what about the last sculpture? When will you complete it?"

Evgeni said, "It is already complete, even though you can't see it. I expect that when you leave for your destination tomorrow, I will begin to use my tools to shape it so that it will be visible to others. Like I said, I have been waiting for your visit."

That evening we shared a meal together and Evgeni told me I would leave for my trip in the morning. He set a round wooden box on the table and asked that I open it.

I opened the box and removed a bowl that I recognized as the bowl from the classroom that I'd held in my young hands almost fifty years ago. When I held it, I instantly felt the same energy and shape in my hands as I had when the professor told me to know it fully. I remembered the professor's words:

"Examine it carefully. Feel its textures. Memorize its shapes, form, size, and color. Create a perfect representation of the bowl in your mind. Commit it to your memory so that you can recognize it both by how it looks and how it feels. Have your hands be as certain of its qualities as your sight. Tell me when you know it in this way. Tell me when you know it as surely as if you had fashioned it yourself. Tell me when you know it as your own. Take as much time as you'd like."

I thought of the words he wrote to me on that photo:

*The time has come for you to fashion such a bowl. Trust that you have learned enough to accomplish such a task.*

Evgeni said, "I received the box many years ago, and it has been waiting for your arrival. I received a letter with the box. This is for you."

Evgeni handed me the letter. I opened it and recognized Professor Ebkilfgn's handwriting. The letter read,

*The time has come. Fill the bowl with water from the place Evgeni sends you. Professor Ebkilfgn.*

Evgeni gave me my last directions. "Take the bowl with you to the river. Fill it with the water that flows under the stone bridge, and then take the bowl and walk upstream. You will see a large fallen tree that has been petrified and is now like stone. Sit on the tree with your bowl of water."

I asked, "And what then? What comes next?"

Evegeni looked deeply into my eyes. I felt like I could see that invisible force he described in the marble. He said, "There is no more to say, my brother. You will know what to do."

I embraced him as one who had just met a sibling who had been separated since birth. I took the bowl and headed to the river. When I reached the bridge, I noticed how old it was. I wondered if it was one of those ancient bridges that supported the Roman armies as they headed east to new lands.

I filled the bowl with water. Slowly, I walked along the banks of the river, feeling the energy of the filled bowl not only in my hands but in my entire being. I came to the petrified tree and sat down, watching the images of the clouds and sky reflect the water in the bowl.

I thought about all that had taken place in my life, all the turns and unexpected moments. Why should today be any different? I looked around me and imagined everyone who had passed along the road behind me and stopped at the river's edge to quench their thirst.

I looked into the bowl and gently touched its surface using the same finger that had been injured the first time I held it. I saw the reflections of my beloved Penelope, my children, and their children. One by one, all of those whom I had met during my travels, including Evgeni, appeared in the water. Then the water became clear and one final image appeared. It was the professor. I began to weep tears of joy. I knew that it was time to stand up and move farther up the river.

In the distance I spotted a stone structure like the one in Spain and the one in my dream. I followed the silent invitation and walked to the structure before standing under the huge canopy formed by the stone supported by the others. Next to the stones was a plant.

The plant appeared to be dormant. I poured the bowl of water over the plant and then placed the bowl on the ground under the enormous table of stone. Slowly I turned and walked back to Evgeni's home. I was going to look back, but I chose to pause for a moment to look down at the river and admire the land before me. I changed my mind about looking back at the stones and the plant. I could hear the sounds of the birds that were already landing on the new branches of the tree that I knew had just sprung from the sleepy plant. It was time to enjoy the road home, the road that I'd walked for centuries. I followed its curve as if I had walked it every day of my life.

# *AUTHOR'S NOTES*

When I told Ardith I was going to write a different kind of book, I said it was an allegory. She was surprised because I rarely read fiction, but Ardith encouraged me in this writing project as she had in the others. One day she gave me an unexpected gift: The piece of pottery that is shown on the cover of the book.

Ardith contacted Mr. Tony Soares, a Native American potter and flint knapper, who made the pot especially for me according to the ancient methods used to make pottery as taught to him by his grandmother. The biggest collection of his pots is in the Springs Preserve Museum in Las Vegas, Nevada. All of his pots are handmade in Joshua Tree, California using local clays.

Ardith and I took the picture in the Sonoran Desert near our home in Arizona. I could never have imagined a more thoughtful gift because it conveyed her interest in and understanding of my work. Most of all, it was a symbol of her belief in me and her abiding love.

The focus of my books continues to expand. My first book was intended to help those who were using a form of bio-resonance testing called Field Control Therapy (FCT), but my friends told me that the book had a larger audience. My second book was intended to help those who were involved in other therapies, including FCT, in which the importance of intention was applicable to whatever techniques they were using. Again, my friends told me that what was written spoke to a larger audience. This book intends to speak to everyone.

The intention-based testing that is described in my first two books created the structure for this book, as well as many of the details, including the principal characters and travel destinations. I used this method to develop many specific descriptions of the characters and the settings of each chapter.

The book was rapidly growing in size, but something didn't feel right, so I decided to use my intention-based testing methods to determine what should be included and excluded from the final version. This process led to the exclusion of many specific details, and the book quickly got smaller. I think the end result is a story that lacks the detailed descriptions of characters and settings that one often expects in stories, but I concluded that if there was too much attention paid to the details of telling an exciting story, it might detract from the intentions of the book.

I also want to thank my dear friend Tina Adamek for her editorial expertise and thoughtful comments about the book.

All calibrations about the consciousness of the book are excluded for similar reasons.

I hope you enjoy *The Dreams of Ebkilfgn*.

www.ingramcontent.com/pod-product-compliance
Lightning Source LLC
LaVergne TN
LVHW051841080426
835512LV00018B/3009
* 9 7 8 1 9 4 6 1 9 5 9 3 7 *